The Lively Art of Writing
Effecting Style

DATE DUE	

The Lively Art of Writing

Effecting Style

LUCILE VAUGHAN PAYNE

Follett Publishing Company
Editorial Offices: Chicago, Illinois

Regional Offices: Chicago, Illinois
Atlanta, Georgia · Dallas, Texas
Sacramento, California · Warrensburg, Missouri

Contents

1

What's Going On in There?

Consider a small mystery.

Two students, miles apart and unknown to each other, write a paper on the same subject. The students are the same age and the same sex, come from the same general background, and are equally proficient in all the mechanics of writing—spelling, punctuation, and grammar. They are also equally eager to succeed. And they think very much alike—so much alike, in fact, that the ideas they express in their separate papers are almost identical. They even use some of the same examples to illustrate what they mean. And they reach almost identical conclusions.

It would appear, offhand, that the two students have actually written the same paper.

When the two compositions finally come under side-by-side comparison, however, it is immediately apparent that at least one thing about them is drastically different. One is genuinely interesting—lively, easy to follow, a pleasure to read. The other is flat, plodding, lifeless—completely correct but completely boring.

How could it happen?

It would be easy to say it happened simply because one student was smarter than the other. Not so. By every known measurement of intellect, the two were an even match. Maybe the author of the dull paper was tired, or felt too pressured to think clearly, or had a sore toe, or a toothache, or a broken heart. Forget it. Both students were calm, confident, blooming with health, and happy as clams. Something entirely apart from these standard alibis had to explain the extraordinary difference between two papers that said essentially the same thing. And the explanation could be found in only one place: in the writing itself.

So what was going on in the writing? What mysterious "something else" could have been at work in the interesting paper yet entirely absent from the other, even though the meaning was the same in both?

The answer to that question is wrapped up in one word: *style*. The writing of one of the students had it. The other's did not.

Style is the one element, everything else being equal, that can give written language the kind of grace, clarity, and precision that makes reading a pleasure. And a very large part of this pleasure springs from the fact that the reader can sense, behind the written words, a real personality—not a word machine grinding out information just to prove it's on call, but a human being trying to speak to other human beings about something worth sharing.

Style in writing bears no relationship to the word *style* as it is commonly used in connection with the latest fashion in clothes or coiffures or cars or any other popular trend. It is not something you add to your writing, as you might add a new tie to your wardrobe or a new shade of lipstick to your cosmetic case. Style is organic; it is as much a part of you as your voice.

In very large part, in fact, your style in writing *is* your voice. And perhaps the most exciting thing about this voice is that it can be trained to express your thoughts and feelings far more accurately and gracefully than you can express them in spoken language. *Trained* is the key word here. Style in

8

writing is not a gift of nature. It is something you learn. Its study will not—indeed, cannot—teach you to write like anybody else. Rather, it will lead you toward writing your own particular best. And this skill is available to anybody willing to take the trouble to uncover its secrets.

No two writing styles are, or can ever be, exactly alike. All genuinely readable writing, however, has certain elements in common. Your understanding of these elements will help you say better whatever you want to say in writing, regardless of the subject you choose to write about. More important, it will vastly increase your own pleasure in the act of writing. After all, it's even less fun to write plodding, ponderous, poor-mouth prose than it is to read it.

Most of the skills you will be exploring in the pages that follow are considerably different from the "basics" of writing that you have been exposed to ever since you entered school—spelling, punctuation, grammar. If you do not feel secure at this point in all three of these areas, start planning now to catch up. A reasonable competence in all three is essential to the pursuit of style. You should be able at this point to do all the following without unduly heavy breathing:

1. avoid all major mistakes in grammar
2. use every form of punctuation correctly
3. spell at least well enough to locate in the dictionary any word whose spelling or meaning is even slightly in doubt

If those three requirements are bad news, bear up, for here is some good news: You will find grammar and punctuation much easier to comprehend as soon as you begin to work with some of the more general problems of style, and you can bring them under control quickly with the aid of your handbook or grammar text (if you don't have one of these, get one, and keep it within easy reach at all times). Improving your spelling by using the dictionary is good news simply because it means you will be using the dictionary.

And that may be the best news of all, for once you start a real search-and-discovery mission in a good dictionary, you will quickly discover that a dictionary search is a far cry from being the grim, dutiful chore you may have once considered it to be—a task undertaken merely to please a teacher or pass a test. After one good prowl through this wonderfully crowded book in search of the exact meaning of a particular word, or of a synonym that suits your purpose, or of a spelling that won't come back in a circle of red ink, you will forget all about consulting the dictionary as a duty. You will start consulting it for the same reason all writers and other word freaks consult it—for the fun of it. And for the endless astonishments it offers.

And how does one of these wonderful books define style? Like this: "the way in which something is said or done, as distinguished from its substance." That's not a complete definition, but it's enough to provide a perfect first step toward understanding one of the least understood elements of style. Note particularly those first seven words: *the way in which something is said.*

Said. That's the key word. If something is said, we can safely assume it is meant to be heard. It makes a sound. Your ears respond to it.

Hold that thought.

Where Style Begins

If you hope to achieve a writing style capable of capturing the genuine interest of anybody at all, with the possible exception of your best friend or your mother, perhaps the first thing you must recognize is this: Your writing must sound right. And sounding right begins when you learn to put sentences together in a way that sounds as easy and natural as friendly conversation.

Writing is always heard. Not merely seen. *Heard.* Reading is not an act of mere seeing; it is also an act of listening. Hear this question? Of course you do. Reading is listening.

In effect, every time you put any kind of message or complete thought in writing—job application, love letter, book report, complaint, criticism, comment, anything composed of connected sentences designed to be read by somebody other than yourself—you are actually setting up a conversation with a reader. This conversation differs in only one important respect from an actual face-to-face encounter: as the writer, you do all the talking. The reader does all the listening. Or so you hope.

It is a situation fraught with a certain amount of peril.

In a real-life conversation, you can expect even very reluctant, obviously bored listeners to be reasonably polite when you insist upon doing *all* the talking. Their eyes may glaze, but they will probably restrain themselves from hitting you in the mouth. Readers are not so courteous. They are fully capable, in fact, of stuffing you into the nearest wastebasket as soon as they lose interest in what you have to say—and whistling as they leave the room. And you can do nothing whatever about it. You can't grab readers by the elbow, or bribe them with offers of refreshments, or chain them to their chairs, or mesmerize them with your magnetic eyes. Once you have lost their interest, they cannot be forced to give you any further attention.

Only one thing can persuade them to hear you out: the pleasure of your company. If they enjoy listening to what you have to say with those written words—that is, if it sounds right—they will probably stick around until you have finished saying it. Otherwise, they are out the door and around the corner, totally unconcerned with the fact that they haven't heard a word you had to say on paper.

That's not a happy ending, certainly, considering the time and effort necessarily invested in any piece of writing. But if you want to be sure of escaping a similar cutoff of communication in writing, you must face the question that every writer ultimately faces: *How can I make my writing sound right?*

You are on the right track when you begin to accept fully the idea that because people read with their ears as well as with their eyes, you must make it possible for a silent reader to *hear* what you have to say. That means giving your written language the easy, natural, "right" sound of friendly conversation.

This "right" sound is, rather obviously, not the only thing necessary for written language to arouse and hold a reader's interest. A great many other factors are involved in that process. But an understanding of just what "right" sound means, and how it can be achieved, is the first step toward achieving the kind of friendly ease that always marks a clear and readable writing style.

Does this mean you should write sentences exactly like those you use in ordinary speech? Heaven forbid. Actual conversation, "realtalk," is so heavily dependent for its meaning upon gestures, volume, tone, accent, facial expression, and dozens of other variables that it simply won't work as straight transcription. And that's putting it mildly. To put it bluntly, if you write exactly the way you talk, your writing is almost certain to sound painfully silly and/or affected and/or downright moronic. And this is true of almost everybody, regardless of age, profession, mental capacity, or expertise with tape recorders. The curious truth is that even though writing should *sound* as easy and natural as real, ordinary talk, it cannot *be* ordinary talk.

How, then, can that easy, natural sound be achieved? *By using, in your written sentences, the natural rhythms of ordinary speech.* Not the actual words. Not necessarily the same subject matter. And certainly not the er-ahs, um-yehs, hey-man-lemme-sees, you-knows, like-I-means, and similar bits of linguistic lint that tend to sift into the cracks of most spoken language. Just the rhythm. Only the rhythm.

And what is the rhythm of speech? Bend an ear to the following examples of realtalk, paying special attention to the natural, uneven, constantly changing pattern of sound created by the speaking voice in each case:

Example 1:
"Okay, okay. I'll see what I can do about it. But I wish somebody else would take a little bit of responsibility for some of this stuff. Including you. You haven't exactly broken your back to help out around here, Buster, in case you think I haven't noticed."

Example 2:

"There, that does it. Now stay right there until I can get a reading from the guys on the other side. For Pete's sake, don't move that marker. If you do, the whole thing will be out of kilter, and we'll be here another two hours. That's it, hold it. Okay, here goes."

Example 3:

"All I know is that everything seemed to be okay when we talked about it at the meeting last month. In fact, they seemed really excited about the way things were going, and I got the impression that they were positive things would work out. Now, *kaboom.* I wonder what happened."

Quite obviously, these examples represent realtalk, that is, words spoken aloud directly to one or more persons. To an actual on-the-spot listener who could see the speaker, their meaning would be quite clear. In written form, they make little or no sense; it is impossible, in fact, to determine from the written words just what the speaker in each case is talking about.

Nevertheless, their sound is clearly the sound of spoken language, and it is this sound that is needed in writing. But if you can't successfully transfer the actual words and sentences of realtalk to written language, what can you possibly borrow from it to improve your writing style?

One thing, and one thing only: its rhythm. The rhythm of talk—the constant variation in sentence length and emphasis that characterizes all spoken English.

Checking the Rhythm

Take another look at those three examples of realtalk. Each is apparently spoken by a different person, and each apparently deals with a different subject. What can these three snippets of realtalk possibly have in common except that they all represent completely ordinary, obviously "real" language spoken aloud, with complete naturalness?

Look a little closer. All three examples, different as they are, have one particular characteristic in common: *the length of the sentences spoken in each example varies constantly throughout.*

That is the rhythm of speech. That's the way you talk—the way everybody talks. In short sentences and long sentences and medium sentences and immensely long sentences and sentences short as pistol shots—the lengths all mixed up, falling wherever the voice naturally distributes them, constantly changing and shifting to fit the meaning of the speaker at the moment of speaking. That's the rhythm of speech, and it is the one characteristic of speech that you can transfer successfully to written language—indeed, it is the one characteristic that you *must* transfer to your writing if it is to sound right.

Fortunately, the transfer is easy once you begin to think of your writing as something a reader will actually hear. In the meantime, or as a double check on rhythm, take advantage of the "paragraph scheme," a device that can give you an instant picture of sentence lengths.

A paragraph scheme is simply a series of lines representing the relative length of each sentence in a given paragraph. Such a scheme based on each of the three examples on pages 12–13, for instance, would look like this:

Example 1:

‾‾‾ · ‾‾‾‾‾‾ · ‾‾‾‾‾‾‾‾‾‾ ·
‾‾‾ · ‾‾‾‾‾‾‾‾‾‾‾‾‾ ·

Example 2:

‾‾‾‾ · ‾‾‾‾‾‾‾ · ‾‾‾‾ ·
‾‾‾‾‾‾‾‾‾ · ‾‾‾ · ‾‾‾‾ ·

Example 3:

‾‾‾‾‾‾‾‾‾‾ · ‾‾‾‾ ·
‾‾‾‾‾‾‾‾‾ · ‾‾ · ‾‾‾‾ ·

Notice that the order in which the various sentence lengths appear is different in each example. If you had twenty or a hundred paragraphs, each would probably be different from all the others. How long or how short any sentence is depends entirely upon (1) what makes the most sense and (2) what sounds right. The two almost always go together.

The sound of any two paragraphs, even when they deal with the same subject, will be different for different writers, just as it is different in spoken language (no two people speak exactly alike, even when they think very much alike). But one element is the same in all spoken English: the irregular, constantly shifting rhythm that fits precisely the meaning of the speaker.

The same thing is true of all writing that sounds right.

The paragraph scheme offers one way to run a quick check on your writing rhythm. It will not guarantee a completely natural sound, but it's a very handy device when you can't actually test your sound by reading aloud (when you are taking an essay test requiring silence, for example). For all other occasions, the best way to test the sound of anything you write is to read it aloud.

Whenever possible, read every paragraph you write aloud—*aloud,* ALOUD—before you declare it finished. Better yet, listen to it while somebody else reads it aloud (this puts at least a small check on your natural tenderness toward your own prose). Much of the work of writing is simply listening. So *listen.* If all your sentences are almost the same length, you will hear the drone. If some particular phrase doesn't quite make sense, you will hear its peculiarity. If the reader stumbles over a sentence, or looks confused, or fails to give some special emphasis you intended, you can be reasonably sure that some kind of change is needed. And the odds are that your ears, those wonderful watchdogs of writing, will provide you with the best and quickest guide to the kind of change needed.

In a word, listen to your writing. *Listen.* LISTEN. Your ears can open your eyes in amazing ways.

CHECKPOINT 1

Read the following paragraph aloud, coming to a full stop at every period to make sure you hear it exactly as it is written:

> I had an extremely enjoyable time at the class picnic.
> Many games were played by those in attendance. A

great deal of food was available. It was quite delicious-looking. It was also quite delicious to the taste. After the serving of the food there was group singing. This was the most enjoyable feature of all. We sang many of the "golden oldies" and at the same time observed the moon as it came up over the water. Everybody considered the outing a great success.

If this paragraph has, in your opinion, the easy, natural sound of spoken language, better have your ears checked.

Rewrite it, from beginning to end, so that it has a more natural sound. Feel free to make any changes you consider necessary to create a natural speaking rhythm or to improve upon the paragraph as a whole in any other way, but do not change the meaning or the actual facts. In other words, say the same thing, but say it better.

To make sure you have a variety of sentence lengths, draw a paragraph scheme of your final version. It should contain at least one example of each of the three sentence lengths: short, medium, long.

Finally, read your version aloud. It should sound better than the original. Does it?

Let's Get Specific

If you have completed Checkpoint 1 according to all instructions provided so far, and if you are trying consciously to establish the habit of listening to everything you write, you are probably beginning to get in some measure the feel of writing in the natural, uneven, constantly changing rhythm of realtalk.

You have no doubt cleaned up most of the worst offenses to the ear that appeared in the picnic paragraph—these tend to get dumped in a hurry when you begin to write in the natural rhythms of realtalk. Chances are, however, that you are still dissatisfied with your own version. You probably feel that it's better than the original—but not enough better. And chances are you're right.

If so, what can you do about it?

16

Take another look at your version. You may have missed one possibility of enormous value in improving almost any piece of writing: *the use of specific detail rather than vague generalities.*

For example: "Many games were played. . . ." What games? "A great deal of food was available." What food, specifically? And what do you mean by *was available?* Let the reader *see* the food; to say that it "was available" makes it invisible. Where was it? Precisely what was it? For all the reader knows, it could have been mush, cooked in steel vats and served out of spigots. "We sang many of the 'golden oldies.'" Which ones, precisely? Name a few. And must you really refer to them with that tired old expression *golden oldies?* They are old songs, that's all. So call them that.

Time out here for a special style note: Always avoid— *always,* ALWAYS—any expression that you have ever heard in an advertisement or seen displayed on a record album. That kind of TV-tainted, discount-house vocabulary will, like baby talk (when spoken or written by nonbabies) and all similarly repulsive cutesy-pie language, turn any self-respecting reader off instantly.

The important thing to keep in mind is that readers like to *see* (as well as hear) what you are talking about. They don't want to be told about "a great deal" of "available" food. They want a fast shot of a picnic table laden with great brown crocks of baked beans, platters of steaming hot-dogs, baskets spilling over with big red apples and purple plums and clusters of fat black cherries. They want *specifics.* And they want color. (How many people do you know who prefer black-and-white TV to color?) Never underestimate the power of color in writing. Use it. And be specific about it.

In short, *show* what you mean. Don't merely "tell about." *Show.* Show with specific details that readers can *see*—in color, when possible.

CHECKPOINT 2

(Read through the entire content of this checkpoint before you begin.)

Rewrite the following brief description so that any reader could *see* what you are talking about. Use both of the stylistic devices you have tried so far: a variety of sentence lengths and specific details that *show* what you mean. Do not repeat any sentence as it now stands. Your object is to say the same thing but to *show* it as well, using color, texture, and specific details:

> Gerstmeyer Technical High School was very old. It was also quite a large building. It was built of red brick. Certain aspects of it were reminiscent of a castle. It made a very strong impression on me as a child. It was only a few blocks from our house. The area in which I lived was very poor and run down. A majority of the residents were unemployed. Things were very hard for everybody. However, it was a real psychological uplift to have a castle in the neighborhood.

If you can recognize how poor a paragraph this is, you are already on the way to improved writing. The paragraph tells about something; it *shows* nothing at all. In your rewrite, *show* what is meant. Show oldness. Show castlelike characteristics. Show the specific details that demonstrate that a neighborhood is poor and run down, that people are out of work, that things are hard. Don't tell what you mean. *Show* it. Use your imagination. You have never seen Gerstmeyer Technical High School, but you can make up "real" details that would look castlelike to a child.

Your description may run more than one paragraph when you really get into the swing of it. Fine. Just be sure to maintain the rhythm of talk—that is, constant variation in sentence length—throughout. If in doubt, check your work with a paragraph scheme.

Finally, read your paragraph aloud. If it still doesn't quite sound right, keep tinkering with it until you are satisfied with the result.

Paragraph Technique

You are probably already familiar with the how-to of building a standard paragraph, but let's take no chances. It's a skill too important to be left to chance.

The sentences in paragraphs do not fall into place automatically. Paragraphs are *built*. They are built according to a plan, or blueprint, that is as simple as it is practical:

> The first sentence of a standard paragraph states the topic; that is, it tells what the paragraph will be about.
>
> The middle sentences explain or illustrate the topic sentence.
>
> The final sentence wraps up the message with a closing statement of some kind, usually closely related to the first sentence.

Simple? It could hardly be simpler. It reflects almost exactly the method you use unconsciously every time you carry on a conversation. For example:

> "That was a great game. I thought for a minute there, during the ninth inning, that our team would blow it, but they really came through. That hit of Dan's did it. I could hardly believe my eyes. He hasn't had a solid hit all season, and whammo, he hits a double with the bases loaded. Then Kathleen Murphey came up with that terrific drive into right field, and that was it. The crowd went absolutely bananas."

Topic: a great game. Middle sentences: the things that made it great. Last sentence: the wrap-up, or summary (if you tie it to the first sentence, omitting all the sentences between, the paragraph still makes sense).

That is standard paragraph organization.

The language used in the example is obviously conversation rather than straight expository writing, but the principle of organization is the same. Once you have tried it a few times in writing, you will find the standard paragraph comes quite naturally to your pen, just as it comes naturally in conversation. As indeed it should. It is, after all, the way your mind works naturally.

The example provided above is a "sequential paragraph"—it tells what happened in sequence. It could very easily be changed from personal conversation into straight prose:

It was a great game. For a few critical minutes during the ninth inning, it appeared that the Blues might have forgotten the proper function of a baseball bat—to hit a baseball—but they finally came through. . . .

The sequential paragraph is one of the easiest to write; its form is dictated by the actual order in which events occur.

The "painterly paragraph" is another much-used model. It is based on the same solid, down-to-earth practical structure that provides the sturdy underpinning for most expository writing: topic sentence, illustration or explanation of topic sentence, conclusion. It is possible, however, to give almost any such paragraph considerably more life and color by approaching it, in effect, as a painter would approach it—with an eye to color, shape, textures.

Suppose, for example, that you choose to describe a particular scene—perhaps a rainy day as it looks from an upstairs window of your school just after the day's last class, as students are leaving for home. Your topic sentence might be simply a brief statement of fact:

It was raining.

How do you develop that kind of sentence into a full paragraph? By using your eyes—and recording what you actually see:

It was raining. Within seconds after the final bell, a river of umbrellas began to flow along the sidewalk below—bright red umbrellas, pink umbrellas, yellow and blue and brown and brilliantly striped umbrellas, floating through the rain like plump, multicolored toadstools. Here and there a big black umbrella joined the crowd, always seeming to move more slowly and sedately than the others, like a fat priest in a holiday parade. On either side of the walkway the grass glistened, every blade heavy with water. The whole world had a wet, silvery look.

Observe that the first and last sentences of this paragraph would make sense without any of the interior details: "It was raining. . . . The whole world had a wet, silvery look."

20

Those two sentences form, in effect, a frame for the picture. The picture itself is framed between the first and last sentences.

Try your hand at it.

CHECKPOINT 3

Write a painterly paragraph at least five sentences long based upon one of the opening sentences suggested here:

1. The day was unmercifully hot.
2. The old house looked deserted.
3. The students were in costume.
4. The car looked like something rescued from the dump.

Develop your paragraph in any way you choose, bearing in mind always the fact that you are selecting details that could actually be seen in a painting (or in a color photograph). Do not make up fanciful, unreal details (or ghosts, witches, hobgoblins, monsters, blobs, and such—these always sound juvenile). Use only genuinely seeable or touchable items that you could reasonably expect to encounter or experience in real life.

Remember to use a variety of sentence lengths, and read your paragraph aloud to make sure it sounds right before you declare it finished.

Your Topic Is Your Key

The kinds of paragraphs you find suggested and illustrated here explore only a minute fraction of the possible topics you might want to develop in writing. A paragraph can do whatever you want it to do—explain, define, enumerate, defend, attack, praise, blame, instruct, analyze, criticize, sermonize, eulogize, categorize, apologize, or simply make you laugh. If that sounds complicated, it isn't. The only thing you really need to remember is this: *The first sentence of any standard paragraph determines what you will do with the rest of the paragraph.*

Take a look at the following sentences:

His name was Xerxes, and he was the best dog I ever knew.

I will never forget my first day at school.

That new TV show is the year's crowning stupidity.

My brother was a self-taught gymnast.

I had a lot of trouble learning to ride a ten-speed.

It was hard for me when my best friend moved away.

My favorite street is Kathryn Avenue.

The worst fight I ever had was with . . .

I still remember . . . , my best friend when I was four years old.

Any one of these perfectly ordinary sentences could easily launch a paragraph. Each paragraph would develop differently, of course, because each subject calls up a different set of memories, and each person's memories would be different from those of anybody else. The principle of paragraph development, however, is the same, regardless of the subject or who happens to be writing about it: All the sentences between the topic sentence and the last sentence either explain or illustrate the topic sentence. The last sentence merely wraps up the paragraph with a statement linked closely to the topic sentence (the two read together, without the central section of the paragraph, would still make sense).

It's really that simple. One of the topic sentences above would require somewhat analytic development, the use of evidence to prove the statement made in the topic sentence. (Pick it out—you can't miss it.) The others require only illustration, or "showing." You have no need to "prove" that Xerxes was a great dog, for example, or that you will never forget your first day of school . You need only *show* Xerxes in the kind of action that proves how great a dog he was, or *show* what happened during your first day of school to make it unforgettable. Whenever possible, do your readers the favor—and the honor—of letting them see for themselves what you mean. Trust them. If you show what you mean clearly enough, they will figure it out for themselves.

All this discussion of topic sentences and paragraph development may strike you as too obvious to require explanation, particularly if you have already studied paragraph development in the lower grades. The fact is, however, that many students tend to freeze up so completely when they face the prospect of writing anything longer than a sentence or two that they forget the obvious. And that can be dangerous to your welfare, for you will always face the necessity of writing at some time, somewhere. And whether the actual task is a school assignment, a college entrance exam, an application for a job, a report to an employer, a complaint, a congratulatory note, a prepared speech, an excuse for tardiness, or a love letter, you need to understand paragraph structure.

So learn it. Get it, once and for all, into your bones and bloodstream. And live much more comfortably, ever after, with pen and paper.

CHECKPOINT 4

Examine again the topic sentences suggested on page 22. Adapt one of these to fit your own experience, or make up one of your own based on experience, and develop a complete paragraph at least seven sentences long in which you employ all the following:

    1. standard paragraph structure

    2. a variety of sentence lengths, including at least one of each of the following:

        a. a very short sentence (5 or fewer words)
        b. a very long sentence (16 or more words)
        c. a medium-length sentence (8 to 15 words)

    3. at least one or two colors that will enable a reader to see something more vividly

You may find it necessary to do considerable rewriting before you meet all these requirements. Hang in there. You will manage it eventually. Read aloud every version you write, checking constantly both the sense of what you say (it must make sense) and the sound (it must sound right).

You are free to use more than seven sentences if you wish (and you will probably find, when you really get into this assignment, that you will so wish). Just be sure to maintain a variation in sentence lengths throughout.

Read your final version aloud to be sure it says what you want it to say—and sounds right. If it fails on either of these counts, start tinkering with it—adding, subtracting, changing, relocating, and generally shoving around words and phrases in every way possible until you get the sound you want. Then read the whole paragraph aloud again. And continue tinkering, and continue reading aloud, until you are fully satisfied that your paragraph makes perfect sense. And *sounds* wonderful.

2

Moving Pictures, Audible Sounds, and Still Shots

Readers are a crochety lot. They don't like to read long-winded passages of description, and they don't want photographs slapped all over every page of everything they read, but they do want to "see" what a writer means. In other words, they want pictures, but they want those pictures to flash on almost as fast as action shown on film. They want pictures that do not call attention to themselves but are simply and suddenly *there*, whammo, straight on, and preferably in motion. Question: How can you make a reader see what you are writing about without actually using photographs or miring down in page after page of description? Answer: You *show* what you mean—with motion-picture and soundtrack verbs.

The more exact the motion or sound you supply with your verbs, the stronger your pictures will be. Observe the difference in the picture quality of these examples:

> A spectacular catch was made by Harry during the ball game.

> Harry raced to the backfield, turned, leaped; the ball smacked solidly into his glove.

Harry hurled himself forward, raised his gloved hand as he hit the dirt, and scooped the ball out of the air.

Look at the verb in the first example: *was made*. It contains only the dimmest kind of picture. Readers are merely being *told* that Harry made a spectacular catch; they are not being *shown*. The other two examples show clearly, through a series of fast-action verbs, just how it happened. *Raced, turned, leaped, smacked, hurled, raised, hit, scooped.* These are motion-picture verbs. They create a far stronger picture in a reader's mind than that flat, colorless, warmed-over, pictureless, gray-spirited verb *was made* in the first example.

You don't need a whole string of verbs, however, to get a motion-picture or sound effect in writing. One is enough to turn a dead sentence into something full of movement or sound—or both:

A cat was seen crossing the yard.
A cat *streaked* across the yard.

The sound of footsteps was heard in the hall.
Footsteps *thudded* along the hall.

The improvement over the dim, muffled verbs *was seen* and *was heard* is instantly apparent. *Was seen* gives you no real idea of what the cat's movement across the yard looked like; *was heard* gives not the slightest hint of the sound the footsteps made. A cat that streaks across a yard, however—or pads, skulks, creeps, limps, or drifts—is a highly visible cat. You could turn a movie camera on that cat and catch its movement exactly. And footsteps that thud—or shuffle, slap, whisper, pound, hammer, or scrape—along a hall are making a real noise. You could put their sound on a soundtrack.

These are motion-picture and soundtrack verbs. Grammarians have other names for them, but the important thing for any writer to remember is the capacity of such verbs to transmit moving pictures and genuine sound. They can electrify dull writing, jolt dead sentences into life, illuminate otherwise dim passages of prose. Your understanding of their function is essential.

Always keep an eye out for verbs containing a motion that could be photographed or a sound that could be picked up on a soundtrack. Or both. Avoid the weak-kneed verbs that transmit only a very feeble picture, or none at all. The fact that a verb indicates motion does not necessarily mean that it will transmit a sharp picture. The motion must be indicated *precisely* if it is to show a clearly visible action. Notice how easy it is to step up the picture power of a verb:

> He went to the door.
> *(No real picture.)*
> He walked to the door.
> *(Only slightly more visible.)*
> He stalked to the door.
> *(Aha! Now we're getting there.)*
> He glided to the door.

Or waddled . . . or reeled . . . or tottered, limped, crawled, tramped, raced, scuttled, staggered, hopped, bounded to the door . . . or got there in any of a great number of other possible ways, any one of them more photographable or hearable than a mere "went." With one well-chosen verb you can, in fact, pack in not only specific movement and/or sound but also instant information: a man who stalks to the door, for example, is probably in a rage.

CHECKPOINT 1

Rewrite each of the sentences below with one or more verbs that increase the visibility and/or the sound of the motion suggested. Do not add any adjectives or adverbs.

1. He sat down.
2. The puppy had a fine time playing in the park.
3. The wind made a loud noise.
4. He left the room in a tremendous hurry.
5. She put the papers in her purse.
6. The garden tiller worked quite efficiently on the hard, rocky soil.

7. She seemed to be feeling very happy when she came into the room.
8. The old man went slowly across the street.
9. The dog lay down on the rug.
10. The boy drank the lemonade very fast.

Animating the Inanimate

In all the preceding examples, the subject of each sentence was actually capable of movement in real life. The really tricky stuff with motion-picture and soundtrack verbs begins when you use subjects that can't reasonably be expected to move at all. For example:

> The freeway exit to Bayshore Drive is on McCurnin Street.

Barring an earthquake or an unusually incompetent construction engineer, a freeway exit is something that does not move. But observe how a motion-picture verb can simultaneously "photograph" that exit and inject new energy into the sentence:

> On McCurnin Street, the freeway exit swoops [or perhaps spirals, or flows, or plummets] down to Bayshore Drive.

This creation of a sense of movement and/or sound, particularly when dealing with inanimate objects, is one of the great games of writing. Again:

> The house was brightly lighted.
> The house bloomed with light.
>
> The fog was so thick that the city was virtually invisible.
> The city swam in fog.

Motion-picture and soundtrack verbs are particularly valuable for shooting new energy into "academic" writing—term papers, literary criticism, history assignments, research in general:

The plot is so complicated that it is almost impossible to follow.

The plot collapses under its own weight.

The writer's style is bad because of too many abstractions.

Abstractions clog every sentence of this writer's work.

Antiwar sentiment was felt all over the country.

Antiwar sentiment swept the country.

Einstein's theory of relativity showed that there was something entirely new in science.

Einstein's theory of relativity crashed through all the old scientific boundaries of space and time.

Collapses, clog, swept, crashed. Could anyone fail to see the difference in pure energy between these verbs and the motionless, colorless, anemic *is, was observed, showed?* If you ever have the uneasy feeling that some of your class papers are dull (a feeling likely to be entirely justified), try giving them a jolt with verbs that force the subjects of your sentences to go into action.

CHECKPOINT 2

All the following sentences tend to be ineffectual because of their verbs. Fit them up with appropriate new motion-picture or soundtrack verbs, changing the wording as necessary to get the effect you want without changing the essential meaning.

1. The room was suddenly full of loud laughter.
2. He finally let the extent of his anger be seen.
3. A startling report was given to the students by the dean.
4. The crowd made disrespectful noises.
5. He made a loud sound indicating disbelief.
6. It was a nice fall day.
7. Pictures appeared on the walls.
8. She was so super-sweet it sort of made you sick.
9. His spirits were very low.
10. Fish were being fried in the skillet.

Using Your Camera Eye

Motion pictures should long since have given you the secret of how to reveal an immense amount of information with one single detail in close focus. A typical shot: a young man standing on a street corner. The camera gives you a rather general idea of what he looks like, but the director wants you to know as quickly as possible a great many other things about this particular young man. So, the camera moves in suddenly to show you certain special details in close-up: first, perhaps, the young man's broken-down shoes; then a button dangling from his coat by a thread; then a tattered paperback thrust into one frayed pocket, with the title of the book visible—*Wild Birds of America*. Not one of these details appears by accident; the director *chose* each of them to tell you something. And every detail relates to the story that will gradually unfold on the screen.

Then, perhaps, the camera shows you where the young man is. It rests briefly on dozens of pairs of feet hurrying across a busy street; swings upward to reveal the facade of a skyscraper; skims along a row of storefronts; picks up a neon sign, a moving bus, a shouting taxi-driver, a cluster of pigeons scrounging through the debris along the curb. Detail after detail makes it clear that the young man is in the busiest part of a very large city. And what is a young man intensely interested in wild birds (remember that paperback?) doing in the heart of a big city? The rest of the film will tell you that, but meantime you have received an enormous amount of information—all of it transmitted through quick shots of carefully selected, highly specific details.

Specific. That is the word to remember. You can, as a writer, transmit information to readers exactly as a film-maker transmits it—through specific details that readers can see. Verbs can give you "action shots." Specific details can supply the "stills"—the camera briefly at rest on a particular object.

Look at the difference in these pictures:

> He liked to read the Bible.
> A worn Bible lay open on his bedside table.

She looked like a rich woman.
A diamond twinkled on her left hand, a ruby glowed on her right, and her clothes had the cut that said money, money, money.

Try your hand at showing (rather than saying) what you mean in the following exercise.

CHECKPOINT 3

Rewrite all the following sentences with specific details that show (rather than tell) what they mean. You may also use motion-picture and soundtrack verbs if they make your pictures stronger. Do not use the word *picture* or *camera* at any time. You *are* the camera.

1. He looked nervous.
2. He was a very interesting-looking man.
3. The yard looked terrible.
4. He was crazy about candy.
5. The dog looked dangerous.
6. The building was in a run-down condition.
7. It was a cold and dreary day.
8. The crowd was getting angry.

Thinking in Pictures

No doubt the main reason that pictures have such universal appeal is the plain fact that we like *seeing*. We spend our lives looking at things, and we are delighted with anything that adds to our capacity to take in the world with our eyes.

But we have another compelling reason for wanting and needing pictures: we *think* with them. Thinking is not some great, foggy marshland in the brain where vague, not-quite-identifiable shapes labeled IDEAS float around. Thinking is far more likely to be a process of sorting out a series of mental pictures we have stored away—pictures of many different but entirely real things. We hold these pictures up in our mind, look at them, compare them, evaluate them, figure out their meaning. We see, therefore we understand—or at least we have some basis for trying to understand.

31

Let's assume, for example, that you are trying to convince the people in your community that water pollution is a serious problem. Which of the following is most likely to convince them?

1. an antipollution speech at City Hall

2. a statistical report on the quality of the drinking water

3. aerial photos of the city's reservoir and sewage treatment plant

4. close-up motion pictures of garbage and dead rats floating in the local water supply

The obvious answer is, of course, Number 4. (If you chose one of the other three, you would appear to be off on a running start for a career—but not as a writer. As a bureaucrat.)

Never underestimate the power of a picture, particularly a picture of something real. Hang on to that word *real*. Few things are more boring than the kind of fanciful effects attempted in certain types of movies—blurred landscapes, misty figures that keep melting into the woodwork, long sequences full of half-glimpsed monsters, blobs that creep under doors, floors that dissolve, unexplained screams in the attic, and all manner of things that go bump in the night. It is the *realness,* the genuine "seeability" of motion pictures that gives them their power. They telegraph their meaning on sight.

Pictures do this on film. And they do it on paper. Never waste your time on the silliness of made-up freakishness in your writing. Let actuality show itself as it is, with absolute accuracy (rest assured that such accuracy can be quite freaky enough to suit any taste). But the thing that gives readers the most pleasure is the sense of reality that pictures can give to writing.

No matter what you think about, pictures are always present in your mind. (You are as defenseless against seeing these pictures as you are against thought itself.) Your problem as a writer is one of selection: Which of the pictures

32

stored away in your mind should you use at any given time?

The easiest and most effective way to make this decision is to think of yourself as a motion-picture camera operator. Then you will be on the lookout, constantly and consciously, for color, movement, striking designs, special textures, vivid contrasts, great close-up shots. This is what all good photographers do; their eyes are trained to see the shots that will say what they want them to say.

That is precisely what you must do as a writer. The only real difference is in the final product: it will be in words rather than on film.

CHECKPOINT 4

Bearing in mind the fact that you are on the lookout for color, movement, textures, good close-ups, and sounds, choose one of the following scenes and make a list of at least ten very specific shots you might take (in color, of course) if you were operating a motion-picture camera. List also at least three sounds you would record on your soundtrack.

    1. a downtown street as it might look to a lost and very scared child
    2. a junkyard
    3. a deserted section of the city
    4. a fight observed from an upstairs window or rooftop
    5. a picnic ground after a big picnic

Working from your list, write three or four paragraphs that show as truly as possible the scene you have selected. Remember, you are *showing* the scene, not telling about it, commenting on it, or judging it.

As usual, remember to emphasize specific details, to vary the length of your sentences, and to use motion-picture and soundtrack verbs wherever possible. And remember: That's color film in your camera. Use it.

3

Special Effects and Assorted Small Hazards

Dialect and Slang

Both dialect and slang are most at home when they appear in spoken rather than written language. When they are used in writing, they can be a real disaster unless they are under strict control. In other words, you must be aware of exactly what you are doing when you try to use either of these elements in your writing.

Sometimes the results are worth it. A hint of dialect or a touch of slang can often add interest and vigor to writing. But, like garlic, these ingredients must be used sparingly. A touch—a very light touch—is enough. Too much spoils the whole dish.

Let's start with dialect. Dialect is simply the way people talk, depending largely upon what region of the country they have lived in most of their lives, or their membership in a particular group within a region. A southerner, for example, may say "you-all" (or "yawl"), a westerner may say "you folks," and variations of the same phrase (like "youse guys" and "you'uns") pop up in certain pockets of the country all the time. Dialect can be interesting and colorful in writing, but it works poorly with "straight stuff"—explanations, descriptions, essays in general—because it's hard to understand when it shows up in cold print. To be effective, it needs the sound of a real voice. So use dialect *only* in dialogue:

> I saw Emmy Lou in her front yard. "Yawl want to come in and have some lemonade?" she asked.

> "Listen, youse guys," said Harry. "Try any funny stuff and I'll bust ya one."

> "I'm real glad to see you folks," said the rancher's wife. "Come on in and set a spell."

Even in written dialogue you must be a bit careful with dialect. If you use too much of it, it becomes too hard to read. You can't expect readers to spend twenty minutes trying to translate something that should be clear at a glance; no reader is interested in working that hard. A word of dialect here and there, an occasional phrase, just enough to give the flavor of a particular region or group (that touch of garlic, remember?) is all you need. Otherwise you will merely antagonize your readers by putting unnecessary obstacles in their path.

You have a little more leeway with slang, but not much. Like dialect, it usually works best in dialogue, and a little goes a long way:

> I asked Joe how he liked the movie. "Far out, man," he said.

Nothing wrong with that. That's the way Joe talks. (He may sound a little old-fashioned now, but Joe grew up in the sixties, when a great many things were far out, real gone, like wow, and groovy.) Slang offers an excellent opportunity to supply a good deal of information about the person who uses it because it's nearly always dated. But slang expressions designed to express your own opinion in straight, or expository, writing can make you sound totally empty-headed:

> The movie I selected for review was *The Clone,* and was it ever weird, wow. I mean it was like really gross. Man, I nearly freaked out when . . .

Cool it, man. It's too much.

The secret of using slang successfully in writing is to spring it on the reader as a swift, small, tongue-in-cheek surprise, a tiny bubble that disappears as quickly as it came. These "bubbles" are particularly effective when they appear in conjunction with otherwise very formal language:

> Mr. Harry Blanchard, the government spokesman, tells us that water pollution can be stopped only if the government takes massive action to stop the polluters. Right on. But what, precisely, is the government doing?

As of this writing, the term "right on" is still a popular slang expression, meaning generally, "That's right; very good; I agree." It is entirely possible, however, that by the time you see these words, "right on" will have been tossed on the linguistic midden where all out-dated slang is eventually discarded. That's one of the problems with written slang; by the time it reaches a reader, it may be hopelessly out of date.

That, however, is not the chief problem with slang. Your writing is probably geared to the present moment, rather than to some misty future, so the fact that slang goes out of date very quickly should not deter you from using it occasionally, particularly in casual writing. The real problem with slang, strangely enough, is its popularity. A slang expression often becomes so popular that it is used to mean almost everything—and therefore winds up meaning almost nothing.

Consider the word *groovy*. It is now definitely past its prime and can probably safely be declared stone-cold dead (millions of people pray so), but not so long ago you could hear that word a hundred times a day in connection with anything that won the approval of the person who happened to be using it. People had groovy personalities, gave groovy parties, served groovy food, had groovy plans, liked nothing better than a groovy movie. Whereupon, of course, the word went instantly out of style. Anybody who used it was labeled at once as a dolt. And not even a groovy dolt.

Slang is invariably picked up by practically everybody who hears it and is then so overused that everybody tires of it in a hurry. In the beginning, it is often fresh and amusing, mainly because it is created in the first place by people with wit and imagination. The very people who create it, however, are the first to get bored with it when it moves into general use. Never assume, therefore, that the use of slang in writing will establish your credentials as a person loaded with wit, sophistication, good humor, or style. It is much more likely—unless you know exactly how to use it—to establish your reputation as a bona fide bore. So use it with great, great care, for special purposes only. And use it very, very sparingly.

This general rule may enable you to keep things under control: Use written slang only as an extremely brief blip in an otherwise serious sentence (particularly a sentence heavy with big, abstract words), and in actual quotations. You are perfectly safe in using quoted slang, provided you quote it accurately and don't overdo it:

> "I can't concern myself with what your friend Zack thinks about the matter. In my opinion, your friend Zack is out to lunch."

> Henry listened to the record twice. He left no doubt of his approval. "Solid, man," he said. "Solid."

Slang always works best as a tiny flash that appears in an otherwise "straight" or serious piece of writing or as a fragment in dialogue and then disappears. Use it thus, and only thus. Then you probably won't go too far wrong.

The following brief description should convince you how completely dreadful a totally slangy approach to writing can be:

> Henry had a really groovy personality like down underneath but he was like uptight when it came to any kind of interpersonal-type relationship. I mean he just never seemed to know where anybody was coming from, and he sort of freaked out when people were upfront about their feelings.

37

One of the curious things about this kind of near-illiteracy, or psychobabble, is its combination of slang with abstractions borrowed from the learned-sounding jargon of psychology. Either of these vocabularies alone—slang or psychobabble—is almost incomprehensible to most readers and is totally repulsive to any person who has any genuine feeling for the English language. The two used together can sometimes be funny, however, so you might as well have a little fun playing around with them.

In case you haven't guessed, your next checkpoint is actually an inoculation exercise. It's designed to let you get all the psychoslang out of your writing system—and to improve your capacity to have fun with it in spoken language.

CHECKPOINT 1

Using every example of psychobabble and current slang that you can recall, write a description either of a character from any novel or short story you have read or of any public figure you have observed on a television talk show (performer, politician, novelist, naturalist, or simply professional talk-show guest). Be sure to include in your analysis words and phrases like *upfront, interpersonal, value judgment, relationship, into* (used in sentences like "He was into fortune telling" or "into orange juice"), and any other currently fashionable jargon borrowed from psychology.

A put-on? Certainly. Have fun with it. And if you ever catch yourself using such terms seriously again, either in conversation or in writing, wash your mouth out with soap.

The Zeugma Game

A zeugma is a figure of speech in which one word is used to modify or govern two or more words although it is used in a different sense with each one. Don't let that rather formidable definition scare you off; the zeugma is actually one of the most amusing devices a writer can play with. (You may find that you like zeugmas so much that you use them too often, so be careful. One is enough for almost any paper.) Here are a few examples:

> He was full of roast beef and good will.
>
> She drove off in a temper and a dusty Ford.
>
> He was deep in thought and debt.
>
> She entered the room in a white dress and a red rage.

See how it works? Give it a try.

CHECKPOINT 2

Complete each of the following sentences with a word that creates a zeugma.

1. The old lady gave him a bowl of soup and a . . .
2. Every time a stranger walked into the store, Mr. Shea raised his eyebrows and his . . .
3. At the secondhand store, Helen managed to locate an old lampstand and a new . . .
4. His mother loaded him up with milk, cookies, and . . .
5. The waiter gave me a clean spoon and a . . .
6. Kathryn arrived in a flurry of laughter and . . .
7. John gave me a piece of candy and a . . .
8. The old man sat in a corner, nursing his grievance and his . . .

Now try a few of your own. You may have to do a few mild mental somersaults to get one that works well, but it's an amusing word game when you get the hang of it.

Parallelisms

One very effective device in the writer's bag of tricks is the parallel structure—a kind of balancing act with language that can give to writing a gleaming finish and a subtle rhythm that can't be achieved in any other way. The easiest way to get a

39

sense of how parallel structure works is to listen to it. For best results, read the following sentences aloud:

1. They talked about the weather, about the scenery, about everything except the problem uppermost in their minds.

2. It was a project that excited him, that challenged him, that taught him a greal deal about himself.

3. She was hot, she was tired, she was furious.

4. He was the kind of man who arrived slowly and carefully at every decision, who never budged once he had made up his mind, who never forgave an enemy.

5. She wanted to go back to the farm, to walk once more through the woods, to wake up in the morning in her old room with the whitewashed walls.

6. If we continue to poison our air and water, if we refuse to give up any of the conveniences of a technological society, if we continue to deny the interdependence of man and nature, we are doomed.

7. To err is human; to forgive, divine.

The parallelism, or "evenness," of the repeated phrases in these examples should be quite obvious: the two people talked about . . . , about . . . , about . . . ; it was a project that . . . , that . . . , that . . . ; she was . . . , she was . . . , she was . . . . This steady recurrence of the same grammatical pattern within a single sentence is called *parallelism*. It sets up a kind of interior rhythm that, for some mysterious reason, is immensely satisfying to a reader's ear.

Examine the parallels in the examples again. Notice that each one is a different kind. In the first one the element repeated is a phrase introduced by the preposition *about*. The second one repeats a *that* clause. The third repeats both the subject and the verb. The final example repeats the *kind* of subject used (in this case, an infinitive): *to err* is the exact grammatical equal of *to forgive*.

Read all the examples aloud, pausing definitely between each of the elements in each parallel structure, just to get the feel of this particular rhythm. Once you get this rhythm into your writing bones, you will probably find yourself using it often and easily, simply because you like the sound of it. Parallelisms of the kind you have been examining appear most often in rather serious writing, perhaps because they have a kind of formal cadence that seems suited to serious themes. But even in the most casual writing, the occasional use of parallelism lends a touch of grace that can lift language above the ordinary.

CHECKPOINT 3

Complete the following sentences with appropriate parallel structures:

1. Suddenly aware of the need to know more about the way city government functioned, Jim found himself going to city council meetings, to . . . , to . . . , to . . .
2. After three months as a hospital volunteer, Jan knew that . . . , that . . . , that . . .
3. Our experience with nuclear power plants in America has demonstrated that . . . , that . . . , that . . .
4. If we do not end war in the world, we may . . .

(The last sentence is a little different from the others; see whether you can figure out an appropriate parallel.)

Similes and Metaphors

Similes and metaphors provide quick, vivid pictures in writing. Both create comparisons: the simile uses *as, as though, as if,* or *like* to set up a comparison; a metaphor jumps straight to the comparison.

Simile:

> The man was as big as an ox.
> The street looked as though [or as if] a hurricane had hit it.
> They sang like a choir of slightly offkey angels.

41

Metaphor:

> The man was an ox.
>
> The street was a disaster area.
>
> A choir of slightly offkey angels from the first grade provided the music.

These are very simple similes and metaphors. Much more exciting—and more effective—are the pictures that can compress more complicated meanings into a single image:

Simple statement:

> Hundreds of seagulls were sitting in rows on the beach.

Simile:

> Hundreds of seagulls, sitting in session like congressmen, occupied the beach.

Metaphor:

> A congress of seagulls was in session on the beach.

The secret of any metaphor or simile lies in the fact that the things compared are very different from each other in most respects—sometimes startlingly different—but very much alike in one or a certain few respects. Seagulls sitting in large groups on beaches, for example, actually do look like a congress—more or less lined up, more or less solemn looking, carrying on occasional discussions among themselves, and obviously convinced that they are absolute owners of the space they are inhabiting. The fact that actual members of Congress are unlikely to have feathers or to scavenge the beaches for food is beside the point; the group of sitting seagulls *reminds* a viewer of a congress—or legislature, or parliament, or convention, or congregation. The particular picture you select depends entirely upon what seems to fit as far as *you* are concerned. If you are the writer, it's your picture—nobody else's. Maybe a group of sitting gulls would remind you of an opening-night audience at a gala performance, or a crowd of shoppers waiting on a big sale day for the doors of a department store to open, or any one of a hundred other possibilities.

That's one of the delights of metaphor and simile. They can be endlessly different. And if they work—if they transmit a "real" picture from the mind of the writer—they can elicit from almost any reader a moment of genuine, startled pleasure. So, if you want to succeed with this kind of figurative language, don't make up metaphors for the sake of metaphors (the result will nearly always be dreadful); instead, relax, let your mind take a look at the pictures that will flow into it in connection with almost any thought, and then choose the picture that best fits your meaning. Then the reader will *see*—as well as hear—what you mean.

CHECKPOINT 4

Rewrite the following sentences so that they express their meaning in a simile or metaphor. Don't forget the power of motion-picture and soundtrack verbs to add even more visible and audible effects to your sentences.

1. The rug was pale yellow and very soft.
2. City pigeons are rather slow and fat, and they don't even bother to get out of your way on the sidewalk.
3. He was a tiny man in a black suit, and he always moved very swiftly and quietly through the halls.
4. The old man's face was pink but very wrinkled.
5. The television screen was blank and gray.
6. He was bald except for two little tufts of black hair that stood out over his ears.

Metaphorical Risks

Whether you use a simile or a metaphor in any given sentence depends entirely upon which of the two pleases you more. One is not necessarily better than the other, and it's usually possible to convert one to the other whenever you like (in fact, it's a good idea to try this frequently, just to see how it works out). Both metaphor and simile, however, do present a couple of hazards that must be guarded against: staleness and "bad mix."

Staleness is the problem with all the old, tried-and-true metaphorical phrases that have been tripping thoughtlessly off your tongue for so long that you have probably forgotten that they are metaphors: "tired as a dog," "sharp as a tack," "He's a rotten apple," "She's a little mouse," "That's the way the cookie crumbles," "seventh heaven," "cloud nine"—an almost endless list of overused phrases that no longer carry even the slightest hint of a real or a surprising comparison.

Even in conversation, worn-out metaphors are tiresome enough to cause any person with a discerning ear to break out in hives; in writing, they are a disaster. Avoid them. Better no metaphor at all than one that has been used so often that it has lost all its power to surprise.

The "bad mix" metaphor (usually called a mixed metaphor) is any metaphor that creates in a reader's mind a picture that is either physically impossible or so grotesque that it is unbelievable. For example:

> The new wave of scientific inventions paved the road to a bright economic future.

Nobody, of course, ever paved anything with a wave. What causes metaphors like this? One thing: the failure of the writer to *visualize* every sentence containing any kind of comparison or contrast. The road paved with a wave would never have survived on paper if its writer had been visualizing the picture those words created.

Always make sure that you can actually see (in your mind's eye) your own metaphors before you put them on paper. Your reader will try to see them, that's certain, for a bad mix tends to create a picture so peculiar that readers struggle especially hard to see what the mix means. The result is often unintentional comedy: "He guided the ship of state through a forest of problems," "We must take a hard look at this invisible enemy," "Let's put our shoulders to the wheel and drive straight for the goalpost," and everybody's favorite howler, "You've buttered your bread—now lie in it."

44

Just for the fun of it, try making up a mixed metaphor of your own. If you find it difficult, fool around for a while with some familiar phrases like "birds of a feather," "tree of life," and "good as gold."

Assorted Small Hazards

Some of the things that go on inside sentences (but shouldn't) are easy to miss. They sound only slightly wrong, just wrong enough to set up a small, not-quite-identifiable but definitely irritating buzz in the ears of most readers. You should be on guard against these errors simply to protect your own interests. It makes no sense to allow minor flaws to mar good work when a moment's attention can prevent that irritation altogether.

The Which-Mire

The word *which* is a very handy term to have around when you need it, and you need it fairly often. Too many *which*'s, however, make a which-mire. A which-mire is a bog of unnecessary words that forces you to flounder about helplessly while your meaning sinks out of sight. Fortunately, it's easy to extricate yourself from a which-mire if you keep your eyes (and your ears) open.

Every time you use a *which,* ask yourself these two questions: (1) "Can I get along without it in this sentence?" (2) "Can I use the word *that* instead of the word *which* in the sentence and still make myself clear?"

If you can get along without the *which* altogether, throw it out. If you can't get along without it, try the word *that* in its place to see whether it fits. If *that* sounds right, use it instead of *which.*

In short, hang on to a *which* only when you are certain that nothing else will work in its place.

CHECKPOINT 6

I. Decide how many of the *which*'s in the sentences below can be eliminated or changed to *that*. Rewrite each sentence accordingly.

1. The notice which he put in the paper on Saturday had his address wrong, which made him very unhappy.
2. She had a horse which was very hard to break.
3. The coat which he wanted to wear, which was exactly the right color, was the one which he had torn at the picnic which he had attended.
4. I don't know which one of you will be allowed to go on the trip which we planned.
5. The car, which was only a year old, began falling apart soon after the trip which the family took.

II. Write a paragraph at least three sentences long describing your left hand. Use the word *which* at least three times in every sentence. The result, of course, will sound ridiculous. That's the point. Maybe you will get all the unnecessary *which*'s out of your system.

Prepositional Dead Ends

Another flaw in writing that shows up frequently enough to send readers up the wall is the overuse of sentences that end with prepositions. Here are a few examples:

> I don't know where my coat's at.
> What did you say that for?
> That's the club he's president of.
> Where are you going to?

At, for, of, and *to* are the worst of the prepositional offenders when they fall at the end of a sentence. They give readers the feeling of having stubbed a toe or tripped over a loose rock. As a matter of fact, that's just about what happens. The prepositions are neither needed nor expected, and that is precisely why they are so annoyingly in the way.

Get rid of them. It's very simple. Each of the four examples could lose its preposition without the slightest twinge:

> I don't know where my coat is.
> I've mislaid my coat.
> I can't remember where I left my coat.
> I can't find my coat.
> Why did you say that?
> He's president of that club.
> That's his club. He's the president.
> Where are you going?

Purists insist that no sentence, ever, should end with a preposition. Practically, that rule makes little sense. Certain prepositional endings are now so firmly embedded in natural speech that they sound peculiar in certain sentences if they are displaced. "Where are you leaving from?" and "Who are you going with?" are two such examples. It would sound quite unnatural in ordinary conversation to ask a friend, "From where are you leaving?" or "With whom are you going?" The only rule covering either usage is common sense: Use the one that sounds best to your own ear.

CHECKPOINT 7

Rewrite the following paragraph to get rid of all the prepositions that appear in awkward positions. Feel free to change the wording any way you like in order to improve the sound, so long as you say essentially the same thing. Remember: Vary the length of your sentences, and check the sound of your paragraph by reading it aloud before you declare it finished.

> The second door down the hall was the one I knocked at. A man answered and asked me what I was there for. I told him about the meeting I wanted him to go to and where it was being held at. He wanted to know why I thought it was a meeting he would be

interested in. I told him about the club I was a member of and the things we were working for, and he finally decided it would be a good meeting to go to.

The There *Fixation*

You have probably worked enough with motion-picture and soundtrack verbs by this time to be aware of their amazing power to bring new life and color to otherwise flat, uninteresting sentences. Nevertheless, you may still be a victim of the *"there* fixation"—the habit of using the expression *there is* in your writing, along with all its forms (*there was, there were, there will be, can be, should be,* and so on). Nothing is wrong grammatically with the use of *there* in this fashion, but something is drastically wrong with it in practical terms: it forces you away from the use of verbs that could make your writing infinitely more alive and interesting.

Consider an example or two. "There was a fire in the fireplace" is neither as direct nor as vivid as "A fire crackled in the fireplace." In the first sentence, readers are *told about* a fire. In the second, they can see and hear that fire themselves, all by virtue of a single verb: *crackled.* Or consider this sentence: "There was a teakettle boiling on the stove." Compare it with this: "The teakettle whistled." If it's whistling, it's boiling. And it is on a hot stove. Readers can hear it, and because they can hear it, they can see it.

Try this one: "There was sudden loud laughter in the room." You could trade that for genuine sound by chopping off that *there was* and making the laughter hearable: "The room exploded with laughter."

The *there is* construction has a way of sneaking unnoticed into writing. The only safe way to stay out of the stylistic sand trap it represents is to *avoid it altogether.* Refuse to use it in any of its forms. This will force you to look for substitutes to put in its place. And your search for a way out will almost always lead you to a better, more vivid way of expressing the same thing. Usually it will direct you toward rearranging the sentence and using a motion-picture or soundtrack verb— which is usually precisely what you needed from the start.

In all but two of the following sentences, you can say the same thing better without using the word *there*. Try it, adjusting wherever and however necessary. Don't limit yourself just to getting rid of the *there*'s and substituting any old verb that works. Feel free to add any details that will improve the sentences, and try for the most vivid motion-picture and soundtrack verbs you can find.

1. There were two cats fighting in the alley.
2. There was a plane roaring overhead.
3. I wanted to help, but there was nothing I could do.
4. There was a really bad fight on the playground yesterday.
5. I'll let you know when I get there.
6. There was a big car coming out of the garage.
7. There is surely something we can do about pollution.
8. Put the trunk over there.

Did you find the two allowable *there*'s?

Passive Voice

The use of passive voice in writing is very much akin to the *there* fixation. Passive voice refers to verbs that require the help of a *was* or *were* as demonstrated in the following examples:

> The car was brought to a fast stop.
> The dishes were being washed.
> The streets were full of people.

All these sentences give a reader only a dim, secondhand glimpse of the action they are supposed to convey. The cure? As usual: motion-picture or soundtrack verbs. Note how much more visible and/or audible the action in the sentences can become when the right verbs begin to operate:

> The car *squealed* to a stop.
> Dishes *rattled* in the sink.
> People *thronged* the streets.

49

These are fairly obvious conversions. Things can get much subtler. Look at the changes in the following:

> The road was built in a circle around the town.
> The road circled the town.
> The car was driven at high speed into the wall.
> The car crashed into the wall.

Notice that each time you change a verb from passive to active voice, the sentence becomes not only sharper and clearer, but shorter. Extra words designed to *tell about* the subject melt away, displaced by one strong verb that *shows* action. And thereupon the sentence becomes instantly clearer, stronger, and livelier.

Passive voice works well as a literary device only when it deals with violent or tragic or completely depersonalized action:

> The man was seized with a fit.
> The driver was killed instantly.
> The building was torn down last summer.

Aside from its use in sentences of this kind, passive voice nearly always indicates excess baggage in a sentence. Dump it. With very little effort, you can convert many a flat, uninteresting sentence into something direct and lively simply by making the subject *do* something—instead of having something told about it.

In short, whenever possible, make the subject of your sentence perform. As the preceding examples illustrate, you can do this even when the subject is an inanimate object.

CHECKPOINT 9

Rewrite each of the following sentences, using the word or words in parentheses as the subject of the sentence.

1. The sound of (the telephone) ringing in the next room was heard.
2. A slight breeze was seen to cause a small movement of (the tree leaves).

3. The sidewalk was covered with (wet leaves). (Do not use the word *covered*.)
4. After (the fire) was started, the room looked more cheerful.

4

Familiar Territory

One dictionary defines an essay as "a short literary composition on a single subject, usually presenting the personal views of the author." That commodious definition could hardly be improved upon as a general guide to writing an essay. It needs to be taken one step further, however, in order to clear up the rather general confusion that surrounds the two terms "formal essay" and "familiar essay."

You are undoubtedly already acquainted with the formal essay. That's the one most students learn to write fairly early because of its practicality; it offers an almost foolproof method of organizing most kinds of classroom papers. Why is it called formal? Because it follows a form: introduction, thesis, body of argument, conclusion. That's what the word *formal* means—*"according to form"*—and that's all it means. It has nothing whatever to do with the tone or style of the essay except in certain kinds of writing that require a highly specialized vocabulary, as in advanced scientific or literary research (both generally incomprehensible to nonspecialists). As a matter of fact, most of the formal essays written today for the general public are distinctly informal in terms of their style—they put forward their "argument" in language as lively and as graceful as possible. So, if you have been laboring under the impression that the word *formal* in writing signifies some kind of stiff-necked, super-proper, heavily dignified tone or special fancy-dress vocabulary, forget it. A formal essay is like a formal anything else: it follows a form.

The familiar essay is much looser than a formal essay, much more personal, and usually much more fun to read. It follows no specific form, no step-by-step plan of organization. Nor does it seek, as the formal essay does, to persuade, advise, instruct, influence, or reason with its readers. It doesn't even try to improve their characters. As a matter of fact, the familiar essay is very much like the kind of story that might come up in the course of any friendly conversation in which one story about a personal experience tends to lead to another. If your friend Evan tells you, for example, about his troubles in the third grade, or your friend Colleen recounts her problems finding a job, you are very likely to respond with a story about some similar experience of your own. "I know just how you feel," you say. "It's like the time I . . ." or "That reminds me of . . ." or "I remember when. . . ." And away you go, summoning up the past effortlessly (and sometimes, rather startlingly, understanding it for the first time or in an entirely new way).

If a familiar essay has one purpose, it is this: to give readers pleasure by sharing with them some experience that has meaning for the writer.

Tuck that word *meaning* back in some corner of your head. We will get to that later.

Using Your Film Bank

Very often a familiar essay springs from a writer's childhood experience. The effectiveness of any written story or anecdote about a childhood experience depends in large part on the "camera eye" of the author. If you think back to people, places, and events in your past, you are likely to see them as pictures, or scenes, that for one reason or another have been caught permanently in your consciousness. These pictures are, of course, your memories—and your memories are your own private film bank. And very often these pictures are *moving* pictures. The dog who followed you everywhere when you were five years old still bounds happily across your mind's screen. The bully you hated still prowls along your sidewalk. Your grandmother still smiles from her chair, the wrinkles breaking across her cheeks like tiny waves.

In a sense, you have been making movies all your life.

Your old movies have one advantage over fresh scenes. They have already been edited (in movie-making, editing is the process of removing all the sections of film that are poorly photographed or meaningless). Time has been your editor; it has erased all the pictures in your mind except the ones that are in some way important to you. You may not even recognize the importance of those that remain, but you may be sure they are important if they are present in your memory. Time is a faultless editor.

Some of your memories may be whole, vivid, moving pictures. Some may be mere flashes—bare hints of pictures that come and go so quickly through your mind that they may seem trivial and meaningless. But if you look long enough and hard enough at one of these flashes, very often it will build into a complete scene.

Recreating such scenes can provide one of the keenest pleasures of writing and the strongest sense of understanding the past. A great deal of writing, in fact, is really just an attempt to get at the meaning of those old private movies by sharing them with somebody—a reader—not simply by telling that reader about something that once happened in your life, but by showing it in pictures. To do this, you need only put those old pictures that are in your mind into words, recounting what happened by *showing* what happened—in color, with motion-picture and soundtrack verbs—and out of all these dimly remembered details a whole memory may finally emerge.

Think back to the years before you started to school. What is the most vivid memory in your mind? Try to *see* it. Think about it until it becomes visible in your mind. The memory can be happy, unhappy, or neither, but it must have in it something visible, whether a person, a place, or a particular object. Close your eyes to see it better. Memories are always more visible behind closed eyelids.

Select only one memory to think about. (You may have a hundred others crowding through your brain, but you must push them aside and concentrate on one only.) When you feel you can see the memory as you might see an actual picture, start thinking about it intensely. Try consciously to fill in details. Keep your eyes closed. Open them only to make notes on the things you see, hear, touch, taste, or smell—faces, movements, voices, objects, colors, textures, plants, animals, everything. No matter how inconsequential a detail seems, list it. Keep digging.

For two or three days, set aside a few minutes just to close your eyes and "see" your memory of the past. Add to your list any new details that show up. Hang on to this list. You will need it later.

Writing from Memory: Two Versions

Following are two examples of a memory that has been recreated in writing. Both deal with the same memory.

Version A:
When I was nine years old, I wanted a BB gun very much. The boy next door had one. My father would not let me have one because in his opinion it was too dangerous. Tim, the boy next door, was two years older than I was and was very good at playing cowboys and therefore inspired in me a lot of admiration. I would often go to his backyard in order to watch him shoot his BB gun. He would shoot at the garage door and was quite good at hitting it.

I thought he might let me shoot the BB gun if I asked

him often enough. However, he would not do this. He said he was a real cowboy, which he could prove by the fact that he always wore cowboy clothes. He said no good cowboy would ever let another person touch his gun. I tried and tried to get my father to buy me a BB gun, but he always said no and even told me to stop playing with Tim. I continued to play with him, however.

One day when we were in his backyard, we heard a noise in the bushes. The noise was made by a bluejay. Tim had always before just shot at the garage door, but when he saw this bluejay he decided to shoot it. It was probably a great surprise to him when he actually hit the bluejay and it fell out of the bush, because he was not really that good a shot. However, he acted like he was some kind of hero and kept bragging about what a great shot he was.

I have always remembered this experience, including the way the dead bluejay looked after it was shot, so I guess it made quite an impression on me. When I went home afterwards I did not tell my folks about what happened. Also I did not go over to Tim's backyard to play after that. I decided that I didn't particularly want a BB gun and stopped asking my father to buy one for me.

Version B:

I guess I never wanted anything as much as I wanted a BB gun when I was about nine years old. Tim, the big kid who lived next door (he was about twelve, so he really seemed big to me) had his own BB gun, and it nearly drove me crazy to watch him pinging away with it, especially when he had on his boots and cowboy hat. He would pull the hat down over his eyes, take two or three steps, turn on his heel, and *pow,* right into the garage door. That door looked like a bad case of acne, it had so much birdshot in it. The thing that drove me crazy was that Tim would never let me try even one shot.

My father wouldn't even listen to me when I asked him for a BB gun. I really tried to wear him down, but not a chance. A BB gun was dangerous, forget about it, shut up. He even gave me orders to stay out of Tim's backyard and to stop playing with him.

Naturally, I didn't pay any attention to that. I kept on sneaking into Tim's backyard every chance I got. One day while I was watching Tim fool around with his gun and going crazy, as usual, with wanting to get my hands on it, a big bluejay landed in the bushes near the fence between our houses. I always liked to watch the bluejays—they're funny birds, always yakking and always up to something, and when they start·swooping around they are about as pretty as anything you could ever see. You just don't expect anything as loud as that, and as alive as that, to be that blue, I guess. Anyway, when I heard the noise in the bush, I turned to look.

I didn't even hear the shot. I just saw the bluejay fall. It came rustling down through the bush and landed on the ground a few feet from where I was standing. It was dead.

Tim let out a whoop and started jumping up and down, laughing and waving his gun and shouting like a crazy person, "Hey, lookit, perfect shot, perfect shot!" I squatted down on the grass beside the jay. One of its wings was spread out like a blue fan, and I put my finger out and touched it. I kept thinking maybe it would get up in a minute and fly away, but I sort of knew it wouldn't. Its eyes were all wrong. They seemed to be open, but they had a queer, dusty look.

Tim shoved the jay with the toe of his boot and bragged some more about his great shot. I couldn't think of anything to say. I just stayed there for a long time. After a while I got up and went home. I never told my folks about the dead bird, but after that I stayed out of Tim's backyard. I just didn't feel like playing with him any longer. And I never again asked my father to buy me a BB gun.

CHECKPOINT 2

Which of the two versions above makes you feel that you can actually see what the writer is describing? Which examples make you understand the writer's feelings more clearly? Which of the two versions sounds more like natural spoken language?

Make a list of at least five instances in which one version "tells about" something, with five matching examples from the other version that *show* the same thing.

CHECKPOINT 3

Now is the time to make use of the list you prepared for Checkpoint 1. Write an essay based on the experience that you selected from your childhood, using your list of specific details as a guide to making that experience visible and real to a reader. In other words, *show* what happened; don't merely tell about it.

What Does *Meaning* Mean?

Although a perfectly remembered and perfectly recapitulated experience from childhood may be a familiar essay, it is not *necessarily* a familiar essay. It may turn out to be merely a description—possibly a very good description—rather than a familiar essay. The difference between the two is contained in the word *meaning*. A familiar essay that has meaning will always relate in some way to something larger than the individual experience that serves as its subject.

Because you are acutely aware of racial discrimination today, for example, you can look back at a past experience and understand it in ways that were not possible for you at the time. Perhaps you were deeply hurt as a child, for example, by something somebody said to you, or by some act of deliberate cruelty. Or perhaps you did something hurtful yourself—chased the "foreign kid" off the street, or picked a fight with a child whose color or religion or manner of dress was "different." At the time, if you were the victim, you may have been aware only of feeling hurt; if you were the one who behaved cruelly, you may have been aware only of your own feelings of power and self-righteousness. When you look back at the experience now, however, you can see it as an example of racial prejudice, religious prejudice, or plain snobbery. And when you write about it, you are actually *illustrating an idea.*

In other words, your essay will not be simply about having your feelings hurt or about hurting the feelings of somebody else. It will be about the evil effects of racial or religious prejudice. And this meaning comes through without ever being put into words. Such words as *racial, prejudice,* and *snobbery* never appear. Your story speaks for itself.

Take another example. You are undoubtedly very much aware today of environmental problems. Let's say you have a writing assignment requiring you to describe some scene you remember from your childhood, and you choose to describe a small park where you once played. So you close your eyes and begin to look at the pictures your mind pulls up instantly from the past, along with a host of other remembered details: the damp smell of the earth after a rain, the flash of color in the dresses of little girls skipping rope, the white hair and wrinkled faces of old men and women feeding the pigeons or sitting on park benches in the sun, the splash of cold water on your face when you doused it at the drinking fountain after a game of tag, the arrogance and elegance of a gray squirrel perched on a tree limb, . . . These details, or a dozen others, swarm into your mind, preserved in that enormous picture gallery inside your head, your memory.

The park no longer exists. It is buried under the ramp of a freeway exit. Only your memory of it—a happy memory—remains. So, when you are required to write a paper based on a memory, you choose the park.

But why this particular memory? Do you choose it just because it happens to be a happy one, and it's there in your head? No. You write about it because, consciously or unconsciously, you are trying to express an idea, perhaps several ideas. You are saying, indirectly, that contact with nature is important, that so-called progress can be ugly and dehumanizing, that natural environments should be preserved and treasured. Your reader can make this connection without any open statement of it on your part if you end your happy recollection with a simple statement of fact:

> Today I watched the cars going up the ramp where the park used to be. I counted fifty cars in seven minutes. It is three miles to the nearest green place where kids can play.

Notice that this ending says not one word about progress or dehumanization or the need to protect the environment. Nevertheless, all these ideas are present in the paragraph—behind the scenes, invisible, but present. Suppose you had ended your reminiscence like this:

> A concrete ramp has been built in the space where the park was. I think it is terrible that kids don't have this park to play in now. Something ought to be done to stop all this destruction of the natural environment. Kids ought to have a chance to see real nature once in a while. The environment should not be ruined for them just so cars can go faster.

Which of the two endings do you prefer?

CHECKPOINT 4

I. Write a brief paragraph explaining your reasons for preferring one version of the park paragraph to the other. Be specific.

II. Suppose you wanted to illustrate the famous Pogo saying, "We have met the enemy, and he is us." What experience have you had, either a long time ago or recently, that could illustrate this statement? Could you make the point clear without ever quoting the statement? Visualize a scene that would express the idea in the quotation. Write this scene in one paragraph.

The Behind-the-Scenes Idea

Every piece of prose that has any real meaning has at its base some central idea. In a formal essay, this central idea is stated openly; it is the guiding thesis of the whole composition. In a familiar essay, the central idea should *never* be stated openly. Rather, it should always be behind the scenes, available to any reader who understands what you mean without having it spelled out. And it is your job to make sure that your reader does understand what you mean. How do you manage that? By *showing*—not explaining, not "telling about," but *showing*—what you mean.

You can discover these central ideas very often simply by writing about the past. If you look long enough and carefully enough at any experience that has been important to you, the idea that it represents will almost irresistibly make its presence known. And in the process, you are almost certain to make new discoveries both about the idea and about yourself.

You need not, however, start with a memory and allow it to lead you to a basic or behind-the-scenes idea to write about. You can start with some personal conviction and then find something in your own life to illustrate it. (This is the method you used when you tried your hand at illustrating, from personal experience, the famous words of Pogo.) The fact is that you can't very well be alive and functioning in today's world—whether you are seventeen years old or seventy—without being involved in, or touched by, or at least aware of, a whole host of concerns that affect the lives of everybody: air and water pollution, ecology, environment, overpopulation, divorce, drug abuse, crime, racial prejudice, equal rights, educational policies, housing, government regulation, juvenile delinquency, divorce, welfare, . . . The terms may seem dry and forbidding, but they are actually pulsing with human life, with individual experience and feelings. People problems. That's what all big social issues are—people problems.

And because you are people, you experience these problems, or most of them, one way or another. Most of them are problems that few people discuss or argue reasonably. They are problems that people live. And it is this life stuff that you want to get at in your writing—your own personal experience in relation to these problems, remembered and examined.

You may find it hard to see how your own experience—the experiences of one solitary person far from the sources of political or economic power—can have much relation to such huge human problems. Actually, it's very easy to make the relationship if you use that invaluable asset in your head—that private picture gallery, that museum of old movies—your memory. If you look hard enough at any great social issue, you cannot help but find in your own life some experience that relates to it. And such experiences are worth writing about—not because they solve any problem (they don't) but simply because they happened and are, therefore, a part of you. Here, for example, are a few of the ways one student might take notes that begin with the recognition of a large social issue and then translate that issue into an individual experience:

Ecology:
My mother considers herself a terrific gardener (biggest and best flowers on the street). Mr. X, the old man across the way buries all his garbage in his yard, never uses a hose (only an old watering can), yàrd looks pretty bad. He caught Mom using a pesticide on her roses, raised cain with her, said she ought to plant onions and marigolds instead of using chemicals to control bugs. Also gave her a long lecture on wasting water. She was furious. But she bought a watering can. And she sent me over to the old man's house with a bunch of roses.

Environment:
Summer. I was 12. Jason and I got all fired up about cleaning up the trash along Marky Road. Terrifically serious about it. Really thought we'd clean all six miles of it in half a day. Got up early. Filled two sacks apiece in less than an hour: beer cans, pop bottles, rusty tin cans, paper cups, one ear muff (?!!), couple of magazines, candy wrappers, orange rinds, a split inner tube. Tired and hot. Left sacks in ditch, went to get ice cream, forgot all about the sacks.

Housing:
Best house we ever lived in when I was a kid: huge old red brick in awful shape, needed every kind of repair, but it had inside wooden shutters and a great winding staircase. Practically falling down, but grand to me. I was 9, felt like a duchess. Actually poor; Pop out of work a long time, not much to eat. But what a house. Pop said it was solid, could be fixed by anybody with a little money and be good as new or better, and last forever. I went back to see it last summer. It was gone. There's a hamburger stand where it used to be. I don't think anybody in there felt like a duchess.

The challenge of writing from an idea base is in attempting to *show* (not merely "tell about," but actually *show*) what you mean without actually stating the meaning. Prepare yourself to find out how it works right now.

CHECKPOINT 5

Select from the following list two statements that you believe to be true. For each of these points, write one paragraph describing something you have observed or that you have done personally that could be used to illustrate the point in writing. In other words, *show* what you mean. Don't explain it. Don't offer any kind of analysis. *Show* your meaning in a picture of some kind—something seeable that any reader will understand without added comment.

1. People should not be judged by the way they dress.
2. Women still are not fully liberated.
3. Everybody should work to conserve energy.
4. Drug use is dangerous and stupid.
5. People feel better if they belong to a group.
6. A really strong person doesn't need a group.
7. Old people have a hard time in our society.
8. Adults should act like adults.

Remember that your only task is to illustrate the point made by each of the two sentences you select. Don't explain. Don't advise. Don't preach. Don't discuss. Don't point a moral. Just show what you mean, as a camera might show it, in a single picture.

The Old Human Truths

Whenever you write about a personal experience, you need to keep in mind at all times the basic idea, or behind-the-scenes meaning, that you want to express. This idea need not be related to any current social problem. It can be simply a basic belief about human nature.

Certain old human truths (or what we accept as human truths) are so much a part of our thinking that we very seldom really question them or, for that matter, realize how large a part they play in our thinking. Many of them—in fact, most of them—can be found in old sayings, proverbs, or Biblical quotations. "Money is the root of all evil," for example, or "The grass is always greener on the other side of the fence," or even such homely and humorous old saws as "You can lead a horse to water, but you can't make him drink." All such sayings can be richly illustrated with real experiences in the lives of most people.

The old truths that we are all familiar with have hundreds of variations. Writers are constantly "proving" such points as these: that human nature is neither all good nor all bad; that time always brings change; that nobody can ever remain completely innocent; that growing up is a painful process; that cruelty often comes disguised as kindness; that material possessions can never satisfy the deepest human needs; that old age is not necessarily wiser than youth (nor the reverse); that there are in human nature such things as kindness, compassion, courage, and generosity, just as there are such things as cruelty, revenge, cowardice, and greed; that hope springs eternal.

These are just a few of the old truths that shape our view of life, our attitudes, our acts. They are old because they have proved to be true through centuries of human living. They represent the distilled wisdom of the human race. And they are, in the final analysis, what we mean by the word *meaning* in life or in literature.

Everything we read or write, if it has genuine meaning, can be translated into one or more of these simple truths.

For example, suppose that you choose to write, as an experiment with memory, about the time you wanted desperately to own some particular object—say a bicycle. You wanted it so much that you were certain you would be completely happy if you got it. All your discontents would vanish, all your problems would be solved. Nothing else mattered to you. You were obsessed with the idea of that bicycle. You slaved for it, saved for it, badgered your parents for it, hated the world for not providing you with it.

Then, finally, you got it.

At that grand instant it seemed to be everything you wanted it to be. For a whole week you careened around the neighborhood in a state of bliss. Maybe longer than a week. A month, possibly. But little by little the bicycle turned into an ordinary possession. Riding it was not all pleasure, nor did owning it make all your problems disappear. It was just something you owned—finally, something that rusted in the rain and got a flat tire occasionally, something that had to be taken care of, just another *thing*—still nice to have, yes, but not the center of your life.

Which of the old truths does such an experience illustrate? Several: that material possessions cannot fulfill the deepest needs, that innocence is always lost (nothing is more innocent than the belief that one thing eagerly desired can bring final happiness), that time always brings change, that nothing is perfect.

Suppose further that in your efforts to get your bicycle you had made life miserable for your family; you were sullen, rude, snappish, sometimes a crybaby. Or you stole the grocery money to help pay for the bicycle, or cheated your little brother out of his allowance, or refused to buy your little sister a birthday present, or took advantage of your best friend in some way, just to make your dream come true. All right. How do you feel a few months later, when you finally own the bicycle and discover that it is not quite as wonderful as you expected it to be?

You are likely to feel that it cost you far too much, that self-respect is too high a price to pay for anything at all. Another old truth, another meaning.

Search almost any experience you have ever had, and you will find that it represents either some old truth about human nature or some belief you hold to be true about the society you live in, or both. It is this truth that gives your writing depth and meaning. Without it, you have only a collection of words, an empty description.

Let the Experience Speak for Itself

Obviously it would be foolish to write up a personal experience like the one with the bicycle as a formal, logical paper full of closely reasoned arguments. There is nothing to argue about. Something happened, and you learned something from it. That's all. The message will come through loud and clear without ever being stated directly. The experience speaks for itself.

It is almost never wise, in a piece of writing that deals with personal experience, to state your behind-the-scenes idea. Readers don't want writers to tell them what an experience means, to have a moral drawn for them. They want to be left alone to read purely for their own pleasure, to satisfy their curiosity about what happened, and ultimately to figure out what it all means for themselves. The minute any reader catches you pinning a moral tag or an explanation to your personal experience (". . . and that is how I learned the importance of being kind to animals," for example, or "This experience taught me that home is where the heart is," or any one of several hundred other homilies), that reader will feel like throwing up. Or throwing your manuscript on the floor and stamping on it. And with good reason. Readers can become very hostile when you intrude on their pleasure by patronizing them and insulting their intelligence—which is precisely what you do when you tell them something they can see quite clearly for themselves.

In any paper about a personal experience, keep your message to yourself. It should always be present in the back of your mind, but it should never be stated outright or suggested in coy hints. (Actually, coy hints are more repulsive than an outright message; stay clear of both.) Never preach. Never draw obvious morals. Simply show the experience. It will speak for itself. Trust your reader to understand its meaning.

CHECKPOINT 6

Since different writers approach their subject in different ways, depending upon which method seems better suited to their talents, two different ways of beginning this assignment are suggested in the following two plans (A and B). Look them over, decide which is more to your liking, then proceed.

A. Select one of the "human truths" mentioned on page 64, and ask yourself what personal experience you have had—either recently or a long time ago—that would illustrate this truth. It need not be an experience in which you were deeply involved; it can be something you have merely observed rather closely. Write it up so that any stranger reading it could "see" it. Do not at any time state openly the point you are trying to make. Don't explain what you think it means. Just show what happened.

B. Choose any personal experience that you would like to write about, without deciding in advance what kind of point you want to make. After you have selected the experience, ask yourself whether it could be used to illustrate one of the "human truths" mentioned on page 64, or some similar truth. If you can think of no way to use the experience to illustrate such a truth, discard it as a subject for this experiment, and choose another experience.

When you have finally settled on this experience, write one short sentence that states the truth, or basic idea, you plan to illustrate. Put this sentence on a card, or a piece of paper, phrased in this way: "The experience presented in this paper illustrates my belief that . . ." When you have worked out this sentence—but not before—write up the experience. Do not, repeat *do not,* include your guiding sentence in your final paper.

If you remember to use all the stylistic techniques you have learned so far, whichever plan you choose, well and good. If not, do not dismay. In either case, you must now go back to the beginning and check to make sure you can answer Yes to *all* the following questions:

> 1. Have you used a variety of sentence lengths in every paragraph in order to give your sentences the natural sound of spoken language?

2. Have you used motion-picture and/or soundtrack verbs whenever possible?

3. Have you used your "camera eye" in order to give your reader specific details, including exact colors, that show what you are talking about? (Pay special attention to this one.)

4. Have you avoided *all* the assorted small hazards and metaphorical risks mentioned in Chapter 3? (Don't give an easy Yes answer to this question. *Check your manuscript.*)

Look Back and Laugh

Almost everybody facing the prospect of writing about a personal experience tends to get extremely solemn about it. It's natural. We all take ourselves pretty seriously—particularly where our feelings are concerned—and we are all at least a little afraid of looking ridiculous. One of the hardest things in the world to do is to laugh at yourself.

Without at least some measure of this ability, however, anything you write about a personal experience runs the risk of becoming much too heavy. As a result, your readers are likely to get the impression that your whole purpose is to prove what a wonderful and virtuous person you are, how fine and serious and misunderstood and long-suffering and generally admirable. This, of course, moves them to instant hatred.

The writer dealing with a personal experience must always guard against three things: (1) self-pity (the Poor-little-me Effect), (2) self-importance (the Ain't-I-wonderful Effect), and (3) self-righteousness (the Look-how-right-I-was Effect). Even in their mildest manifestations, these are deadly qualities in real life, and they are equally deadly in writing.

Fortunately, you can avoid them all. You have a good start on this plan as soon as you begin *showing* in your writing whatever you want your readers to know (not merely "telling about" but *showing*), thus letting them judge for themselves how you feel about things. Meantime, you might as well try your hand at another—and very amusing—way to attack the problem.

CHECKPOINT 7

Think of some relatively minor episode in your past that made you feel extremely sorry for yourself, extremely romantic, or extremely self-satisfied. (Don't try this with a very recent such experience. It's hard to make a joke of something that hasn't had time to simmer down.) The whole point of the exercise is to overdo it. Remember, it must be a fairly minor episode, nothing life-threatening, nothing genuinely tragic.

Write up the experience as though you really believe it to be the most painful, the most unfair, the most heartrendingly romantic, the most self-sacrificial, the most tragic event in the history of the world. Exaggerate everything. Exaggerate most particularly your own virtues. Exaggerate the faults of everybody else. Overstate every feeling. Suffer all over the place. Wallow in self-pity. If somebody hurt your feelings, don't grieve silently. Cry out with the pain of it. If somebody compliments you, brag about it unmercifully. If you feel romantic, tremble with huge passions. Point out at every opportunity how wonderful you are, or how unappreciated, or how misunderstood. Pour it on.

A spoof? Of course. But you must be careful never to let your reader know you are spoofing. Pretend throughout that you are completely serious.

While you are doing all this, don't forget what you have learned about *showing* your reader what you mean. Be very specific about the details you use (not "He hit me with something that hurt a lot," but "He hit me alongside the head with his waterproof Timex."). But above all, keep your tone throughout completely serious. Heavily serious. Impossibly serious.

The result will probably crack you up. That's its purpose. If it also cracks up your classmates, you can consider yourself a howling success. And you will probably never again make the mistake of overstating your emotions.

"Whoever sets pen to paper . . ."

Writing about personal experience always carries with it the danger of self-justification or self-aggrandizement, and these characteristics are as tiresome in writing as they are in conversation. Now that you have had a chance to get them out of your system by laughing at yourself, you should be able to handle almost any personal experience in writing without bogging down in descriptions of your feelings. Instead, you will *show* what you mean—and who you are. Readers don't want to hear you discuss your feelings. In fact, they will almost certainly turn sour if you proffer self-analysis of any kind. They want to make their own analysis, thank you, and decide for themselves just what kind of person you are.

But how do you tell them that? Do you try to describe yourself with statements like "I am a friendly person" or "I am extremely shy" or "I am the kind of person who . . ."? No. Never. That tells readers nothing except your opinion of yourself. Invariably, even though you may be the most modest and unassuming person in the world, such self-description sounds impossibly conceited. What readers want is a chance to form their own opinion of you; they have no interest in hearing yours.

The only way you can present yourself truly as the living, breathing, complicated person you really are, is by writing about some subject that interests you intensely. It hardly matters what the subject is. As E. B. White, perhaps the most beloved of all modern American essayists, has said, "Whoever sets pen to paper writes of himself, whether knowingly or not." Remember that. Your ideas, your opinions, your memories, your feelings—all these *are* you. Choose any subject, and they will permeate everything you write.

CHECKPOINT 8

The range of subjects for a familiar essay is endless. But if you need a few specific ideas to get started, you may find something useful in the following list of possible titles. Some may mean nothing at all to you. Others may remind you of something in your own experience. Those are the ones to concentrate on. Choose the one that brings to mind most strongly some experience that you can use to illustrate it. Think in pictures. Use your memory. Search for the one important truth you can illustrate. Then write.

Unplanned Things	You Can't Take It with You
I'll Call You	The Subway
What's In a Name?	The Politician
Sports Headlines	Song Titles
The TV Slave	The Crack in the Sidewalk
Street Fight	Don't Crowd Me
Yoga	The Accident
Liberated	Pay Day
Hair	Crowds
At the Zoo	First Job
Choices	Running
Books	The Visit
Ownership	I Remember
The Winner	Social Security
The Motorcycle	The Bus
The Good Friend	A Room of My Own

5

The Reviewer's Stand

Almost everybody likes to talk about movies and television. In fact, part of the pleasure in seeing anything on the "tube" or in a movie theater comes from *re*-viewing it—seeing it again inside your own head, taking a second look at the pictures your mind has stored away. During this period of recall you very probably compare what you have just seen with similar shows you have seen. And if the show was, in your opinion, good enough or bad enough to deserve any further attention, you are likely to discuss it with your friends. Or argue about it, if you disagree. To see a movie or a major TV show without talking about it afterward would probably seem downright unnatural.

In effect, when you think about a movie or a TV show you have seen, you are actually *seeing it again*. This re-viewing, however, takes place only in your mind. Your memory supplies the pictures, sounds, colors, and movements that particularly pleased or displeased you. You won't remember every detail, of course, but you will remember a great deal.

Very often it is only after this second "interiorized" viewing that you feel sure of your opinion of what you have seen. Why? Because it is very difficult to think analytically about a movie or a TV show while you are watching it. The personal beauty or charm of the performers may momentarily blind you to shortcomings in story or characterization. The sheer power of the lights, color, music, and dance of a "spectacular," or variety show, can often sweep everything before it, including most viewers' logical thought processes, artistic standards, and plain good sense.

To arrive at a genuine opinion (not an impression, or a feeling) you need to look *again*, to *re*-view mentally what you have seen. Only then can you properly sort out your thoughts and pin down the specific qualities that you can judge intelligently as good, bad, or indifferent.

Sometimes, of course, a TV show or a movie is such obvious claptrap—both poorly conceived and badly performed—that it deserves no attention whatever. In such cases, a quick hand at the dial and a short memory are your most valuable assets. But when a show does manage to rise a few degrees above the awful, as happens on occasion, most of us suspend our final judgment until we get outside the theater or far enough away from the TV set to think about what we have seen. We have a headful of pictures to examine slowly and quietly, away from the noise and color of the actual show.

All sorts of surprising things can happen during this "second look," or re-viewing period, particularly in reference to movies. A minor character may emerge as the most interesting character of all—perhaps because of a superior performance, perhaps because of better writing on the part of the dramatist. A story that seemed entirely believable while you watched it unfold on film may strike you after re-viewing it in your head as plain silly or totally false. Or a scene that puzzled you, or seemed pointless when you watched, may suddenly make sense.

When any of these things happen, it probably means that you are beginning to think like a writer. You see why the writer wrote the scene, what it was designed to accomplish in terms of plot or character development.

Your re-viewing will undoubtedly also make you more

sharply aware of certain technical aspects of a film. You may realize that although you liked the story, you were annoyed by the blurred "mystery" shots, or by the soundtrack, or by the color, or by certain weak performances, or by any number of other elements that contributed to the total effect of the film.

In short, whether you like a particular film or whether you hate it, you usually enjoy thinking about it, comparing your impressions with those of other people who have seen it, running it through your mind again—re-viewing it. If you organized your thoughts and put them down on paper, you would have a piece of writing called a movie review or a television review.

An informal style and a strongly personal tone are perfectly suited to such reviews, for your entire personality is involved when you pass judgment on popular entertainment. That's one reason reviews are fun to read and sometimes even more fun to write. Furthermore, the interest of readers is practically guaranteed. Few of us can resist reading a written opinion about anything that we have witnessed, read, or taken part in. We may disagree with the written opinion. We may even be thrown into a purple rage by it. But we want to know what it is. Writing as popular as this demands an informal, personalized style. The subject is usually controversial enough to generate excitement, familiar enough to require a conversational tone.

Writing such reviews can do more than improve your writing skills; it can sharpen your perception of just exactly what you are looking at when your eyes are on that movie or TV screen. You will be aware, while you are watching it, that you cannot get by in writing with a mere emotional response that might pass muster in conversation—a "Wow, that was really a great show!" or an "Oh, brother, was that ever dumb." When you sit down finally to write, you must be ready to give very good reasons for your opinions—*specific* reasons based on *specific* evidence from the show itself and on certain standards that any movie or TV show must meet in order to merit serious consideration. You must be able to make comparisons with similar productions, you must be able to defend your point of view logically, and you must do all these things in a writing style that readers will enjoy reading even though they may disagree with you.

CHECKPOINT 1

Select for class discussion a movie or a television show that all or most of the class has recently seen. If you can watch something together as a group, so much the better. It is likely that some of you will enjoy the show, some will hate it, others will rest their opinions somewhere between these extremes. Work together as a group to formulate a list of all the elements that should be included in making an intelligent judgment of the particular show you have all seen. You may disagree about what these elements should be. You can work that out. Just keep in mind that the elements to be included will depend to a great extent upon the kind of film or show you have seen. Obviously, you won't judge a talk show the same way you would judge a documentary film about life on the Hong Kong waterfront. As a general rule, your list should include everything that the makers of the film or television show did with sight and sound to sway your thoughts and emotions.

When you have agreed upon the elements to be considered, divide into two groups, with half the class working out a list of reasons for believing the show to be worthwhile and effective and the others a list of reasons for believing it to fail in one or more ways. If all of you liked the show, the job of finding something wrong with it can become quite a challenge. And vice versa.

You will not be asked to write a review—yet. But what you learn from your discussion of pros and cons right now will be invaluable to you later. So give the discussion your best shot before proceeding further.

Selecting a Subject for Review

In all likelihood, you see so many television programs, so many old movies on TV, and so many made-for-TV movies that the selection of a subject for a review can be a problem. How do you make a choice?

Your best bet, as far as movies are concerned, is the made-for-TV movies. A great many of these, unfortunately, are obvious junk, worth neither the close attention required for a genuine review nor the time to write one. Now and then, however, a made-for-TV movie with a first-rate script and outstanding performances does make an appearance on network television. Such movies, certainly, are worth reviewing.

So are certain other programs on television. Some network series shows that appear again and again, year after year, are worth reviewing simply because of their longevity. What is it about them that makes them perennially popular? Answer that question, and you automatically have a review on your hands. Compare a new series with an old series; again you have a review.

Perhaps the best way to select any movie or series or special program for review is this: Simply choose the one that has affected you strongly enough to make you want to express your opinion of it, either pro or con.

The Review Form

A review of any kind (whether of a movie, a book, a play, a concert, or anything else that merits a written critique) is actually nothing more nor less than your old friend, the formal essay (the kind of essay that follows a definite form). You have probably used this form dozens of times to express your opinion on a whole range of subjects, but a reminder of just how it works may be helpful when you try your hand at a review.

The form (or structure, as it is sometimes called) of a formal essay consists of three main parts:

> 1. An introductory paragraph that lets the reader know in the first few sentences what the essay is about, ending with one sentence that states the *thesis* of the essay. (The thesis is the main point that the essay will

seek to "prove" or at least present in a persuasive way.)

2. A "body" consisting of several paragraphs that support the thesis with evidence and/or various logical arguments.

3. A final paragraph that briefly summarizes the argument in favor of the thesis and makes a concluding statement that clearly wraps up the subject.

Your first step in writing a review is choosing your thesis. Everything hangs on that. Until you are very clear about your thesis—the main point you want to make—you can't expect to write a genuine review. So let's examine that problem.

Establishing Your Thesis

Basically, a review is a criticism. (*Criticism,* by the way, does not mean a mere search for flaws or the expression of purely negative thoughts. It means the art of making *discriminating judgments,* pointing out both good and bad points in the work being reviewed.) In effect, when you write a review, you are saying, "I have judged this work [movie, TV special, documentary, book, play, concert] against a valid set of standards for all such productions, and I have arrived at the following opinion." The opinion may be favorable or unfavorable, or a little of both, but it must be an *opinion,* not a purely emotional or spur-of-the-moment reaction.

This opinion is your thesis.

It is not enough, in other words, to claim as a thesis a mere throwaway comment like, "This was a terrific movie; I loved every minute of it." Or "The 'Bertie Bingle Show' is really dumb." Comments of this kind are meaningless; they come off the top of everybody's head without the slightest thought. They are literally not worth the effort it would take to write them down. The thesis of a review must be arrived at through careful thought and genuine analysis, for it is the position you must defend and support with evidence drawn from the movie or program itself.

77

Once you have established your thesis, your procedure is precisely the same as the procedure for any formal essay: beginning with an introductory paragraph. This paragraph lets the reader know what you intend to discuss and ends with your statement of thesis. Follow that simple prescription and you can't go wrong. But one word of warning is in order: *Keep this introductory paragraph brief.* One thing no reader wants to hear is a long, detailed review of plot. If you have ever sat through a long-winded friend's blow-by-blow description of a movie, you know how infuriating this can be. Always wrap up the plot of a movie in one or two sentences, or even in a single phrase:

> *Daffodil Lane,* the story of a young girl's attempt to escape the cruelties of city life through an imaginary existence in a world created entirely in her own mind, . . .
>
> *The Flimby Case,* a harrowing film about intrigue and revenge in the suburbs, . . .
>
> *Beyond the Blue,* a string of more-or-less related episodes in the life of a paint salesman, . . .

End your brief summary of the plot with a brief statement of your thesis—your opinion as to whether the film succeeds, does not succeed, succeeds only in part, or deserves to be hooted into permanent oblivion. Or you might offer any one of a hundred other possible opinions. Then, following your thesis, you will proceed to comment on all or most of the following elements: the basic idea behind the film, the acting, the pace (Does the story move along quickly, or does it seem to drag?), the dialogue (Does it sound right? Does it hold your interest? What is its purpose?), and the photography and soundtrack.*

You need not follow this particular order, of course. You may want to open your review with what you consider the most effective element in the film—or its worst fault—and let

---

*You will discover many, many more elements to be considered as you look more and more closely at television and motion-picture offerings, but these will get you started.

78

your opinions branch out from there. Or you may want to start with an entirely different kind of introduction—an anecdote perhaps, a quotation from the film, a bit of information about the writer, director, or producer. How you begin a review is entirely a matter of personal choice. The one thing you must bear in mind is the fact that you are actually writing a formal essay. This means that you are writing an essay that follows a specific form and that you must build it accordingly: introduction, thesis, pro and con arguments, conclusion.

Before you try your hand at writing your first review, read a few reviews written by professional critics. Old movies present a special opportunity. If they are "serious" movies (meaning movies that are serious attempts at art) you can be reasonably certain that they have already been reviewed by the best professional reviewers in the country, either in the major news magazines or in a select few magazines of high literary quality. Search out a few. You'll learn more about reviewing movies in general—and learn it faster—by reading a few first-rate reviews of old movies than you could learn in any other way. Furthermore, you could have a great time doing it. Good reviews are very good reading indeed—sharp, penetrating, often wonderfully funny, and nearly always illuminating.

Let's be clear about one thing, however. You will not find genuine reviews in movie magazines, and you certainly will not find them in the pulps that crowd newsstands and display racks at grocery checkout counters. These are mostly scandal sheets, lurid tabloids full of alleged "inside stuff" from Hollywood. Most of the gossip, of course, is fiction dreamed up at the desk of some cynical hack writer, and any alleged movie reviews are not reviews at all. They are simply overheated advertising copy known in the trade as "hypes," designed specifically to attract foolish customers to poor movies. In short, sucker bait.

Don't expect to learn anything about writing reviews (or writing anything else) from publications of this kind. Read them if you must. They won't necessarily cause brain rot, even though they are fairly certain eventually to induce acute nausea. But if you do read this trash, at least take care to balance it with an equal amount of genuine, first-rate critical writing about movies.

The review section of any major news magazine is a good place to start. If you want to go beyond that but don't know where to look, consult your librarian. Librarians, in case you haven't learned this yet, are the best friends any writer, student or professional, can ever have. They know almost everything there is to know about anything in print, including where to find it. And helping you find what you want is not only their business but their great pleasure. Wonderful people, librarians.

CHECKPOINT 2

What do you consider the most interesting movie you have seen during the past six months? (Do not include for consideration cartoons, disaster movies, movies about pet animals, or exploitative movies of any kind.)

What main idea about life or about human beings or about human institutions do you think your selection expressed? Formulate a thesis based on the movie's success or failure in relation to this main idea. Then write a review explaining and illustrating your thesis with evidence drawn from the movie itself. Take another look at the elements listed on page 78 if you need a reminder on what to cover.

New Worlds to Conquer

Now for the best part.

For some curious reason, very little that could be called genuine reviewing of television programs exists in the United States today. Possibly the reason for its remarkable absence lies in the fact that TV is so widespread and so taken for granted in today's world that it is treated in much the same way the weather is treated: it may be good or rotten, but we accept it as it is. After all, there isn't much we can do about the weather. The same thing, however, cannot be said about television. A great deal can be done about the programs offered by the mighty TV industry, and it can be done with a relatively small, hand-held instrument known as a pen. Or a pencil. Or a slightly larger instrument known as a typewriter. Any one of these three tools, guided only by a cool, inquiring, determined mind could bring about improvements in television that nothing else has been able to accomplish.

The fact is that a body of intelligent, thoughtful, serious, forthright, written opinion about television in all its aspects would command enormous reader interest. Such a body of opinion would concern itself not only with movies but with *all* television programming—variety shows, documentaries, talk shows, series shows, public service programs, advertising, sports coverage, political commentary, news, personalities, everything that the television industry brings into the modern home at the touch of a switch.

Such a body of opinion does not exist today. Sooner or later, it is bound to come.

Let's start it here.

CHECKPOINT 3

Select from the four types of shows on the following list one nationally televised program that you dislike intensely:

1. a game show that gives away expensive prizes or large amounts of money

2. a talk show consisting mainly of casual conversation between a host and various "show biz" personalities

3. a "talent" show in which contestants compete to win prizes for having the least talent

4. a contest in which participants are required to compete against each other in foolish or humiliating ways

Then establish your thesis (the main point you want to make about the show). Make sure it is specific enough to handle in a short paper. You cannot possibly prove, for example, that any show is the world's worst *or* the world's best in four or five paragraphs. And don't content yourself with hurling critical adjectives at the show you select—*rotten, stupid, degrading, self-serving,* and such. Leave the adjectives out. *Show,* with specific examples, what is rotten, stupid, degrading, and so on.

Write your first rough draft of this essay as fast as you can get it on paper. Don't worry about fine points of style. Just get everything out of your system as fast as possible. Then let your paper cool at least overnight while you give yourself time to think about a writing technique that you might like to try.

The Ironic Touch

Irony is a favorite device of many writers and a source of pleasure for all reasonably sophisticated readers. It can be defined as the use of words to convey the opposite of their apparent meaning. For example:

> Comment by a drenched commuter on a cold, miserable day: "What lovely weather."

> Written comment by a book reviewer about a dull book: "This is a truly restful novel. It will put you to sleep in six minutes."

The ironic touch never calls attention to itself. It appears suddenly and is gone, like a quick, secret smile between two people in a crowded room. It may be no more than the small, pleasant shock brought about by an unexpected relationship between words. For example, where the unskilled writer might use an overworked adjective like *awful,* the ironic writer will speak of a "dedicated bore," an "inspired gossip," an "unswerving coward." And because words like *dedicated, inspired,* and *unswerving* are usually associated with admirable acts or qualities, they provide a minor reversal that pleases because it surprises.

Irony succeeds, of course, only when the reader is in on the secret. In other words, when you say something you don't mean, you must be quite certain your readers know you don't mean it. Your recent paper about a television show you disliked or disapproved of offers you a splendid opportunity to try your hand at irony. Now that your first blast has had a chance to cool off, take another look at the essay you wrote for Checkpoint 3. Does it sound outraged? moralistic? self-righteous? If so—or even if it sounds merely dull—now is the time to try a touch of irony.

It's very easy. You need only pick out at least one element in the show that you particularly disliked and write about it as though it were something you admire. Don't overdo it. A mere flash of irony is always more effective than a long, heavy-handed put-on. If your subject for review was a talk show, for example, you might slip something like this into your review:

> The Willie Glubber talk show offers viewers a splendid opportunity to hear an assortment of television stars express frankly and openly their opinions on such subjects as their favorite foods, their favorite clothes, their favorite hairdressers, their favorite weather, and a host of other equally profound and controversial matters.

Irony seems to praise while actually expressing scorn. The words express the opposite of their literal meaning. If, for example, you chose to review a game show requiring a certain amount of knowledge about language, you would heap praise upon the participant who could successfully spell *cat* and the host who mispronounced only two words. If you chose to review a contest show requiring participants to undergo some kind of humiliation to win money—a pie in the face, a scramble for coins, a race to pile up the most merchandise in a grocery cart, a competition for the least talent—you would of course praise the show for its wit, humanity, good taste, and charm.

CHECKPOINT 4

This checkpoint offers two alternatives. You may choose the one you prefer.

A. Look over the essay you wrote at high speed for Checkpoint 3. This, you recall, was an essay based upon a TV show that you dislike. Does your writing have any touches of irony? If not, if it is deadly serious or completely humorless, rewrite your review in an ironic vein. You may find it hard to treat with humor a show that you genuinely loathe, but give it a try. And remember: Don't overdo it. No heavy-handed insults, no preachiness, no righteous wrath. Just administer the shaft quickly, accurately, and as gracefully as possible.

B. If you have difficulties with irony, you may prefer this alternative assignment. Write a letter to the network that carries the show you dislike, expressing your opinion of it and your reasons for holding such an opinion. Write another brief note to any company that advertises a product on the program.

You need not mail these letters. They are simply an alternative to writing a full ironic essay. The letters can be very brief, but their meaning must be entirely clear. To make sure of this, follow the basic form of the standard essay in the body of the letter. State the point you want to make and follow it with your reasons for feeling as you do.

And Now, the News

How about reviewing the news programs that you see on television?

Let's be realistic about that question. Without a very strong background in history, sociology, modern politics, and journalism, plus a respectable grasp of economics, it would probably be impossible for any reviewer to handle competently a subject as complex as the national news. Even local news programs can present difficulties, for quite often certain journalistic judgments that the viewer cannot recognize are involved in decisions about news programs.

Does that mean, therefore, that such programs are sacred cows, never to be examined or criticized? Far from it.

In one respect, news programs can be and should be prime subjects—if not, indeed, prime targets—for practicing the reviewer's craft. Pictures, after all, are not the only element involved in news programs. To the contrary. The primary ingredient of newscasts is *language*. And it is here, in the use of language, that the one great fault can be found in news programs, particularly local programs (the standard of language usage on national newscasts is generally excellent). On local shows, standards are all too often very low—the language you hear tends to be not only graceless but loaded with plain old-fashioned (and sometimes laughable) errors of usage.

CHECKPOINT 5

All the following examples of newsroom news and newsroom chitchat contain imperfect usage—either outright errors or a meaning that has been muddled in some way. If you were a member of the news staff and were told that you would be fired unless you could remove all the flaws in these examples, what changes would you make?

1. "The governor stated that she was opposed to the new tax. More importantly, she said she would veto the measure if it passed."
2. "The weather report tonight is different than this morning's prediction."
3. "The reason for the change was because some of the committee members complained."
4. "Regarding the strike, increased wages were the main issue."
5. "The scene of the accident was a grocery store in Larsonville, a small community off of the main highway."
6. "The weather is not apt to change much before the weekend."
7. "All of us here at the station will try and give you, our viewers, our very best."
8. "The paintings now hanging in the local art gallery are the most unique display of the year."

9. "The mail that came in this week to Ramona and I really gave us a big lift."

10. "Eight people were killed in the mishap."

11. "Drop by the headquarters anytime this week, and you will receive a free gift if you visit the station."

12. "It's impossible to predict what will happen at this point in time."

13. "All of us are looking for food that has less calories."

14. "It was a very unique situation."

15. "We are not sure of the time frame for this program."

Does Misused Language Matter?

We know that language changes, that what is rejected today may be accepted tomorrow. Does it, then, really matter whether or not the language heard daily on news programs meets accepted standards of appropriate usage?

It matters enormously.

It matters not because "correctness" is in itself a sign of virtue or even of superior intelligence. It matters because, at any given time, the language accepted as standard is likely to be the most efficient and the clearest for most people. It matters because confusion over the meaning of any word in a telecast, or the fuzzing-over of one idea that could be made clear with a moment's effort, is in effect an act of vandalism. It corrupts language. And make no mistake: The corruption of language leads eventually to a loss of human understanding and a devaluation of human experience.

It is the special duty of all professional people involved in communication, particularly those whose actual voices are heard day in and day out, to respect their native language enough to use it exactly, clearly, and with at least some small touch of grace. It is quite certainly *your* right to demand these qualities from people who make their living through *your* ears.

The weird inappropriateness of misused language on programs that quite literally depend for their very existence upon language is, in itself, a made-to-order topic for ironic essay treatment. Other possibilities:

1. the chummy manner and "Hey, good buddy" vocabulary sometimes maintained by the news staff in relation to each other while on the air

2. the interview segment in which the interviewer talks so much that the interviewee has trouble getting a word in edgewise

3. sports announcers who, as they recite a long series of game scores, insist upon using a different verb each time as a substitute for the word *beat* or *defeated*

4. the weather reporter who turns the weather forecast into a kind of vaudeville act, forcing viewers to sit through various "hot-shot" or "personality-kid" routines in order to hear the one thing they want to hear—the weather forecast

5. the verbal padding that shows up all too often even in straightforward weather reports, turning showers into "shower activity," fog into "fog-type conditions," freezing rain into "dangerous driving-type situation," and so forth

Remember, if you try your hand at irony, that your tone must never be angry, indignant, or self-righteous. Stay cool and detached. Make your point with a very small needle, not a sledgehammer.

CHECKPOINT 6

Devote at least one week to listening every day to a local news program on television (the same one every day). Make note of every blunder in word usage that you hear and of every other element in the program that you consider particularly annoying. Make note also of any elements that you consider particularly good.

On the basis of this week's examination, formulate a thesis that expresses your judgment of the program. Then write a brief essay developing your thesis, illustrating it with specific details from your notes. Express yourself throughout as clearly and calmly as possible, using third person only (do not at any time use the personal pronouns *I, me, my,* or *mine*).

Do your best to stay cool. Keep your tone good-tempered if you are highly critical, calmly assured if you think the program deserves praise. Remember throughout to vary constantly the length and structure of your sentences in order to establish the natural rhythm of talk.

TV Needs YOU

It is often easier in writing to attack something objectionable than to defend something that is worthwhile or simply enjoyable. No honest critic, however, can ignore the good things television has to offer. If you are to play the critic's role, you must consider TV's best as well as its worst points.

A curious thing about television is that anyone can take part in it. Anyone—*you*—can participate in television programming. How? By responding to it *in writing*. Television, more than any other industry, is almost immediately responsive to public reaction to its programs. It wants to please. It is seldom eager to take chances, but *it does want to please.* And herein lies your opportunity to become a television critic, an assistant program director, and a public benefactor—all this with a few strokes of your pen or a few thumps on your typewriter. You could hardly find a more satisfying way to put your new writing skills to useful employment.

Obviously, before you can expect to have your opinion considered seriously, you need to bring yourself to the point that you know what you are talking about. The last thing needed by the men and women who run television is further bad advice. They can get plenty of that without leaving their own studios—from "experts" who demonstrate daily that they are contemptuous of most viewers' intelligence and taste. What they need—and what they probably would like very much to have—is informed and judicious criticism.

Will your comments be read, your judgments noted, your ideas considered? Be sure of it. Television's desperate need to please makes that almost certain. And the very fact that you have taken the trouble to write gives your words real influence. One letter is a thousand times more effective than a check mark on a survey or a response to any other impersonal method of registering your opinion. A written criticism carries weight. That's all the more reason to be sure that your own is informed, reasonable, and written with all the skill you can muster.

Give it a try. You may find it the most enjoyable writing experience you have had.

CHECKPOINT 7

To provide a subject for your letter, select a television program that you think may be particularly interesting during the week ahead. Make firm arrangements to "attend" it exactly as a professional critic would attend any theatrical or cultural event—with paper and pen at hand to take fast notes *while you are watching the screen.* Do not wait until the show ends to scribble your comments. Do it as you watch. Be precise about the things you like or dislike.

Immediately after the show, read through all these notes carefully. Don't put this off. The meaning of such rapid notes tends to melt away very fast. These notes are your "evidence." Read them over the instant the show ends. Try to identify your reasons for feeling one way or the other.

Once your notes are clear, establish your thesis. Basically, this will be your opinion of the production you watched, boiled down to one sentence.

Then line up your "evidence," with the good things about the show in one column, the bad in another. If you have more good than bad, you obviously approved of what you saw. If you have more bad than good, you obviously did not approve. (If the balance is even, the show probably was dull.) In your letter, you will support your thesis with the "evidence" in its favor. You will mention the evidence against your thesis, but only briefly. Most of your comments will be devoted to "proving" that your opinion of the production—whether good, bad, or indifferent—is correct.

Your letter, in other words, will actually be an essay that follows the traditional form except for its opening salutation and its "very truly yours" ending. Try to maintain the easy, natural rhythm of spoken language throughout, but avoid all slang and other careless usage. Think of your letter as a friendly message to someone you respect—and who will, you hope, respect you enough to listen to your opinion.

If you feel any confusion about following the standard essay form, take a quick look back at essay structure in *The Lively Art of Writing: Developing Structure*. You have just written a letter. All you need now is an envelope and a stamp. The final step should be obvious.

6

The Irresistible Subject

The one subject that interests more people than any other subject on Earth is other people.

Every other topic for writing pales by comparison. War, revolution, baseball, politics, even money—these subjects are mere spare-time diversions for readers when compared with the universal attraction of a piece of writing that concerns itself with one living, breathing human being. Just one, mind you. Not a crowd. Not even a couple. And certainly not that faceless creature of the computer age, the all-purpose, economy-sized, scientifically cross-sectioned, population-sample-representative-group-norm blip on some screen or dot on a chart. One *real* person. One single, separate, distinct, warts-and-all human being. Alive and (preferably) kicking.

Face it: with the possible exception of secret scribblers who hide their diaries, all writers want to be read. To have an audience. And any writer who can bring another human being to life on paper can be sure of having that audience. It makes very little difference who the human being is—movie star or mail carrier, countess or carhop, truck driver or tap dancer, sky-diver or cat-skinner. If a real person comes through in the writing, readers are hooked. They have met the Irresistible Subject, and they will not be content until they have tracked that subject from the story's first sentence to its last.

What this means to you as a writer is practically everything. You can never run out of material for your writing, for you are surrounded by Irresistible Subjects. You can write in ways that go far beyond the newspaper, with its unadorned presentation of facts. You can even go beyond the pictures and sounds offered by television and movies. You can give readers a living portrait of another human being—and you can do this with the stamp of your own personality on every sentence you write.

It can be the most satisfying experience you will ever have as a writer. Don't expect it to be like anything else you may have tried. It isn't.

The P.I.A. Story

The "personality" story (the story that goes beyond the straight presentation of facts and figures) falls into the general category that became known in the 1960s as the "New Journalism," but it is called by a number of different names—character sketch, in-depth interview, profile, interpretive journalism, literary journalism, personality-in-action piece. Not one of these titles quite hits the mark, for each omits one key element—the writer's own particular "voice," or style. But some kind of handle is necessary, and the one that seems to describe most accurately the actual content of such stories is "personality in action." So call it a P.I.A. story. That's short and handy.

To see the difference between a P.I.A. story and some of the more traditional treatments of the same subject, compare the three approaches below.

A typical news item is brief and to the point. It might read like this:

> William Murphey, a senior at John Nelson High School, has announced the official opening of the

Murphey Household Clean-Up Service, a domestic service specializing in household cleaning jobs. According to Murphey, the all-male crew is prepared to handle every aspect of household cleaning. Other members of the crew are Ray Diethelme and Jerry Kehl.

A typical newspaper feature story might go something like this:

High school senior Bill Murphey sees no reason to wait until graduation to start a career. He has already established a business of his own, the Murphey Household Clean-Up Service, an all-male enterprise specializing in housecleaning chores. Two of his classmates recently signed on with the firm after a six-week training program supervised by Murphey and his mother, Helen Murphey.

How did Murphey, who was runner-up for a state wrestling championship last year, get into the housecleaning business? "I needed a job," says Murphey, "and I couldn't find one anywhere. And I figured that the only thing I could get trained for in a hurry—and for free—was housework. So I sort of apprenticed myself to my mother."

He admits it was rough going for a while. "Housecleaning is really hard work. I couldn't keep up with my mother at first." Eventually, however, Murphey worked out methods of his own that he claims are not only more efficient than his mother's but also easier.

Apparently many local housewives are impressed with the Murphey service. The crew already has so many jobs lined up that no new customers can be accepted until the end of the school year. Are the boys making much money? "We must be," says Murphey. "Look at our sign. It says we're cleaning up."

A typical P.I.A. story would show members of the clean-up team in action, quote them, and attempt to give readers a real sense of the group's methods and of their personalities, particularly Murphey's. It might develop somewhat like this:

MURPHEY'S WHITE SOX—THEY'RE
CLEANING UP

"Hey, Murph!" The voice is loud and male, and it's coming from an upstairs room in a posh house in one of the poshest subdivisions in the city. "How about checkin' me out? I'm through up here."

"Hey, Murph!" Another male voice, this time from the living room. "You wanna look at this stain on the rug? It wasn't here last time."

"Hey, Murph!" It's the upstairs voice again. "Hold the checkout. I need another ten minutes."

Murph himself, William B. Murphey, senior at John Nelson High School and current runner-up for the state high school wrestling championship (148-lb. class), is finishing up his work in the kitchen. He is dressed in an ancient pair of jeans, an equally ancient sweatshirt, and a pair of snow-white socks. He has just finished scrubbing the floor, and he is walking across it now, rubbing it with his feet, stopping to look every few steps at the soles of his socks. They are still clean. He looks pleased.

He also looks very Irish. He has one of those big Irish heads, wide mouth, big ears, a handsome curve of nose, copper-colored hair, fair skin, blue eyes. You can sense the muscles under the sweatshirt. And the ease. He's absolutely at home with himself, relaxed, confident, cheerful. And in charge.

"Man, do I like these self-cleaning ovens," he says. "I'd rather scrub ten floors than clean one oven by hand." He pads across the kitchen, picks up a basket filled with an assortment of cleaning supplies, and walks toward the living room. Ray Diethelme, another wrestler, also wearing white socks, points out the stain on the rug. It's about the size of a 25-cent piece. Murph squats down, runs his fingers through the spot, puts his nose to the floor and sniffs it, brushes the nap with his fingers again. "No problem," he says. "Use the stuff in the blue bottle. The X-16. Brush it on with the toothbrush. *Lightly*. Read the directions first." He leaves the cleaning basket with Diethelme and pads out, heading for the stairs.

Jerry Kehl is coming down the hall, carrying his own basket of cleaning supplies. He's also wearing white socks. Jerry's not a wrestler; he's a track man, and he plays oboe in the school orchestra. He grins at Murph and holds up first one foot, then the other, showing the soles. They're clean. "Okay," says Murph. He steps into the bedroom, runs a finger along the window sills, the tops of the door casings, the surfaces of the two matching chests and the lamp tables. He takes a quick look under the bed. "Sometimes people throw a few things under there just to test us," he says.

Finally he picks up a cardboard box that's sitting on the bed. The word MURPHEY'S is printed in big letters on every side. Murphey examines the contents of the box very carefully. It contains one handkerchief, a recipe clipped from a magazine, a safety pin, a dime, two pennies, a hairnet, and a needle threaded with blue embroidery floss. He returns the box to its place on the bed and heads back for the hall.

"That's it for here," he says, and starts moving faster. All three of the boys meet in the service entrance at the rear of the house, where they remove their aprons and white socks, put on their shoes, and fill out their time sheets. They have spent exactly ninety minutes in this house, doing exactly what they were assigned by the owner. They are leaving every part of it they touched spotless, fresh-smelling, orderly. Within five minutes they are all in Murphey's pickup, on their way to another job in the same neighborhood.

One question nags: What was that box full of junk all about, the one left on the bed? "We never throw anything away," says Murphey, "and we never take anything out of a house that we didn't bring in. Not *anything*. Not a hairpin. Not a paperclip. If people leave stuff around, they will always find it in one of our boxes. Sometimes I think they drop stuff just to test us, to make sure we've done our job. But mostly I want to make certain that nothing—and I mean *nothing*—disappears from a house when my team is in it. Our business is built on trust, and we intend to keep it that way."

Murphey calculates the time for the day's second job at about 45 minutes. It's a small apartment; depending upon what the tenant wants done, they may even get out sooner. The cleaning team left school at 2:00 p.m.—all have special permission for early leave on workdays. That means they can probably be home by 4:30, with the whole evening ahead of them.

Do they like the work?

"If you knew how hard it is to get a job in this town, you'd know how much I like it," says Kehl. "The work's hard, all right, but it's kind of interesting, in a way. And the pay's not bad."

"I like the work," said Ray Diethelme. "No kidding. I think it's interesting. Besides, where else could you find a job where you can run around in your socks all day?"

The socks, like most of the other features of the Murphey operation, are Bill Murphey's idea. "All our indoor work is sock-footed. *White* sock-footed. That's the only way you can be sure a hard-surface floor is clean. Even my mother never thought of that idea."

His mother, Helen Murphey, thought of almost everything else. When her son came up with the idea of a cleaning crew, she put him through the jumps for three months before declaring him fit to clean any house properly. She also turned over to him the old Datsun pickup his father had bought shortly before his death. It now serves as transport for the entire crew and all their gear and supplies.

Is the business really making money? It began breaking even about three months after it began, according to Murphey. He manages now to pay the minimum wage to all members of the team, including himself, to pay all transportation and supply costs—including white socks—and to make a small profit. Not bad, he thinks, for a part-time, shoestring, student venture. He hopes to have a full-time business established by next summer.

Has he thought of hiring girls? A glint of Irish mischief comes into Murphey's eyes. "I'd like to," he says, "but I really don't have time now to train people who don't know anything about housework."

CHECKPOINT 1

Suppose that all three of the preceding stories were available for you to read during a long wait in your dentist's waiting room.

Write a single paragraph answering, in the order given, all three of the following questions:

1. Which of the three stories would be most likely to attract and hold your interest?

2. Why? (Answer this question *specifically,* with evidence drawn from the story itself.)
3. P.I.A. stories always carry a by-line (the name of the author). Why is this desirable or necessary?

The Movable Force

Take another look at the three sample stories on pages 93–96. The necessary information for the first example (straight news story) could have been obtained easily by a telephone call. The second would probably have required a personal interview with Bill Murphey by a reporter who asked questions, jotted down the answers, and limited the final story strictly to the information received. The story includes a few details that supply a slight sense of background, but these details add little or nothing to arouse a reader's interest in the personality of Murphey himself. Nor does the story have the unmistakable stamp of one writer's personal style. It is bland, colorless, basically mechanical; the story does not make Bill Murphey hearable or seeable, nor does it give any real notion of the actual work undertaken by his crew.

Note that in the third example (the P.I.A. story), the same basic facts are still used but the emphasis has changed entirely. The facts have become merely a part of the story. Certainly they are an essential part, but the real story is the *central character in action.* And to get all the detail that made such a story possible, the writer had to do a good deal of moving around—actual, physical moving around—simply to see and hear everything finally selected for use in the story. The writer, in other words, had to become a "movable force," a kind of traveling, on-the-scene, camera-microphone-receiver-transmitter-interpreter, invisible to the reader but always present.

When the Irresistible Subject meets the "movable force," you get the P.I.A. story. Not before. Move you must. No writer ever put together a personality-in-action story by sitting at a desk and dreaming up pretty sentences. To get

97

your net around a P.I.A story, you've got to get up and *move.*

Take another look at the sample P.I.A. story. Check it against the other two stories dealing with the same subject. Identify everything you find—either stated explicitly or merely suggested—that does not appear in the first two examples. The presence of this additional material suggests that the writer's *method* of gathering information was different from the methods used in connection with the other two stories. Identify at least three pieces of information and five visible details that appear in the P.I.A. story but not in the other two stories, and suggest how the author might have obtained these details.

Truth or Fiction?

P.I.A. stories are often so vivid and interesting that readers sometimes suspect that they are reading fiction rather than truth. This is partly because readers are so accustomed to conventional methods of writing about reality that it's easy to suspect that the author of a P.I.A. story is making the whole thing up. This is so widespread a notion that it needs to be spiked immediately.

Everything in a P.I.A. story must be true. Every piece of factual information must be checked for accuracy. Every scrap of conversation that appears in the story and every action shown, however minor, must be genuine. *Everything must be true.* In fact, the power of the P.I.A. story lies exactly here, in the transmission of reality exactly as the author sees it.

The P.I.A. writer's insistence upon accuracy, in fact, is likely to be downright fanatical, and the necessary research is therefore likely to be much more intense than that of the traditional journalist. P.I.A. writers want every fact they can lay their hands on. But they don't stop there. Their goal is to capture the sense and style of a whole personality, a genuine

98

human being with his or her own way of talking, thinking, moving, working, playing, even dressing. Nothing in such stories is faked, nothing invented, nothing disguised.

The importance of this emphasis on truth and exactness cannot be overstated. The excitement of a P.I.A. story lies precisely in the fact that it is *not* made up; that everything in it is the result of close personal observation; that every fact has been checked out; that every word of dialogue has actually been spoken; that every gesture, every color, every movement is real. The instant any author tries to hype up a story with invented "colorful details" or faked "interesting dialogue" or any other such phony rubbish, he or she loses the right to enter P.I.A. country.

Everything must be true. Everything you use in a P.I.A. story must be something you have personally observed or have checked out for accuracy. There are no limits on your imaginative use of language to express the reality you find, but it must be reality you express, not something you invent or falsify simply to create an effect.

Everything must be true. Tattoo that thought on your brain, get it into your nervous system, circulate it through your bloodstream before you start down this trail.

Got that?

Okay. Now comes the question: If *all* fact and specific details and dialogue in a P.I.A. story are taken from real life, why does such a story so often sound like fiction?

Reason: The writer uses fictional techniques. Not fiction itself—everything must be true, remember?—but fictional techniques: action scenes, dialogue, strong visual detail, sharp delineation of character, imaginative use of language. In short, the author takes advantage of the literary devices traditionally used in fiction to dramatize people and events but does so with one critical difference—the P.I.A. author uses these techniques to tell a true story rather than an imaginary one.

In a P.I.A. story, people speak in their own accents. The scenes in which they appear are real, and they show real movement, real colors, real details. The scenes are "fast cuts," changing quickly and dramatically. These are all fictional (and motion-picture) devices. Almost the only device of fiction that you will *not* use in a P.I.A. story is plot. You will have no need for plot; reality *is* your plot. But it is up to you to do everything in your power to bring that reality into focus for your reader.

As many distinguished "new journalists" have long since proved, experience with writing fiction is not necessary to successful use of this method. What it requires above all is the ability to use your eyes and ears to their full capacity and to tell the truth. Not the "plain truth," but the vivid, multifaceted, personally observed, specific, real, and complex truth, always more dramatic and more interesting than any pretty fiction you could possibly invent.

Learning the art of presenting reality in this way begins with tuning up the sensory receiving equipment until every dial is on red alert. The eyes and the ears are the primary receptors. So let's start there.

CHECKPOINT 3

Select one person—a complete stranger, if possible, or at least somebody you know only slightly—and observe this person closely with the idea of writing an accurate physical description. The person you choose must be somebody you can observe at close range for at least ten minutes. During this time, concentrate entirely on what you can see and hear: gestures, features, posture, voice tones, spoken words, clothing, ornamentation (if any), small mannerisms, special characteristics of any kind.

While you observe, take rapid notes. Do this unobtrusively. Jot down specific details as briefly as possible. Avoid all general adjectives. If you see an unusual bracelet, for example, don't note that it's unusual, or weird, or funny-looking, or exotic; instead, make note of *exactly* what it is—a two-inch band of rhinoceros hide, a bunch of braided shoelaces, a collection of dime-store bangles, or whatever. *Al-*

ways make your notes specific. "Nice clothes" means nothing. "Funny nose," "wonderful eyes," "peculiar eyebrows," mean nothing. Be specific. *Show* what it is that makes you think the clothes are nice, the nose funny, the eyes wonderful, the eyebrows peculiar. Don't *tell* prospective readers what you see; *show* them—and let them decide for themselves whether what you show them is funny, wonderful, or peculiar. And don't waste any time worrying about whether a note is "important" or not. The idea at this point is simply to write down as many specific details as possible, not to make judgments about their relative importance.

After ten minutes, stop observing and start writing. Write a paragraph based on the notes, using only those that you judge most likely to create the clearest possible picture of the person you have observed. Avoid such general terms as "neat," "sloppy," "well-dressed," "badly dressed." Be specific. Select details that *show* what you mean.

Then think back. While you observed your subject, you were somewhere—it doesn't matter where, in a classroom or on a bus or at a cafeteria table or at home or in the library, wherever, just somewhere—one definite place. Wherever it was, you saw colors, objects, movements. You heard sounds of some kind. Precisely what colors, objects, movements, sounds? List them (you may find that you remember dozens). List them all. Then pick out from your list at least two of each (colors, objects, movements) that seem to give the best sense of place to the spot where you observed the person you chose as your subject.

Be exact about these details. Again, don't depend upon general adjectives like *noisy, colorful, busy, big,* and *active. Show* what you mean by using precise noises, colors, objects, movements. When you have selected the ones you want to use, scatter them through the paragraph you have already written. Don't put them all together in one great lump. Sneak them in bit by bit, wherever you can make them sound right, either as part of a sentence you have already written or, if necessary, in whole new sentences.

Find the Role, and You'll Find the Action

The first and most obvious step in writing a complete P.I.A. story is selecting the right person as your subject. Personality consists of a great deal more than physical characteristics, speech, or manners. People are what they are not only by virtue of the way they look and sound and impress others but by what they *do*. Most people have some particular activity that defines their role.

Ordinarily, we think only of adults as having roles: teacher, doctor, lawyer, nurse, minister, grocer, secretary, salesperson, merchant, clerk, bus driver, hairdresser, architect, and so on. But students also have roles: gymnast, feminist, model plane builder, math whiz, runner, skier or swimmer or mountain climber, mechanic, dancer, debater, bicyclist, violinist, singer, wrestler, collector, bookworm, letter-to-the-editor writer, painter, seamstress, . . . And that's just a beginning.

The role of a student may be very clear—that of an elected officer or a top athlete, for example—or it may be a kind of "general knowledge" role usually referred to as "Oh, that's the girl who . . ." or "That's the boy who . . ." The activity that follows the *who* is the role: "That's the one who raises hamsters," ". . . who works at the hospital," ". . . who collects insects," ". . . who draws all the posters," ". . . who takes karate lessons," ". . . who makes quilts," ". . . who fights all the time," ". . . who trains dogs," ". . . who jogs ten miles a day," ". . . who . . . ."

Everybody is somebody, and everybody has certain qualities that are special in some way. Therefore, everybody is potentially a P.I.A. subject. It would be possible, in fact, to write an interesting P.I.A. story about the world's most boring, do-nothing dud; the very absence of any central drive might be strange enough to merit investigation. It is a great deal easier, however, and infinitely more interesting for the writer, to write about a person who has some special interest or activity. One person with a single-minded passion for accomplishing anything at all—whether it's skydiving or collecting mushrooms or winning the billiard championship or learning to walk a tightrope—is a hundred times more interesting to write about than a hundred contented "nice guys," male or female, who have no goal beyond being likable.

The more sharply defined the subject's role or major interest, the more interesting the P.I.A. story—and, in most cases, the more interesting the personality. The great advantage for the writer is the opportunity to show the person actually *doing* something—not merely talking about a particular activity but being genuinely involved in it, moving around, handling real objects, getting things done, behaving and speaking with complete naturalness, *showing* a real self in action. And that, of course, is what you are really after.

So, for your first attempt at a P.I.A. story, choose as your subject a person who has some definite role or overriding interest. Do *not* choose, however, a close friend or a personal enemy. The less you know personally about the person you choose as your subject, the better. If you are not acquainted with, or have only a very slight acquaintance with, the person you interview for your P.I.A. story, you can avoid any hint of emotional bias in your work. That's extremely important. Your purpose in writing is neither to praise nor to criticize. It is simply *to show your subject in action.* If you actively like or dislike the person you intend to write about, that person will probably come out looking either like one of civilization's shining lights or like the Enemy of the People. No matter how fair-minded you are, a certain amount of bias is likely to creep into your work. So choose somebody you know only slightly or not at all. Only then can you be positive that you will be able to preserve a completely open mind. Any kind of prejudgment on your part, either pro or con, dooms your efforts at the outset.

This is not the only reason, however, for choosing a stranger or near stranger as your subject. Perhaps the best reason of all is that it's more fun that way. One of the delights of writing a P.I.A. story is the contact it gives you with people you might otherwise never come to know at all, thereby often giving you insight into whole new worlds.

How do you go about getting the cooperation of the person you want to write about? That's the simplest part of the whole business. Ask. If you get turned down, you have lost nothing. Dozens of other potential subjects are always available. Chances are, however, that you will not be turned down. Nearly everybody is pleased by the prospect of being "written up." It is, after all, extremely flattering to be considered interesting enough to be worthy of such attention.

Check Your Private Feelings at the Door

The key factor in a successful P.I.A. story is the interest that the person you write about can arouse in a reader. Readers care nothing about the private opinion that you, in the course of writing your story, may form of the person you are writing about. They will be annoyed, in fact, and justifiably so, if you intrude with your private judgment. Your job is to concentrate all your attention on one problem: how to show your subject in action.

Lay aside all other considerations. It is not your job, as an interviewer, to act as a judge. You are there to *observe*. Think of yourself as a kind of human radar screen, switched on and constantly scanning, a piece of supercharged receiving equipment designed to see, hear, and transmit sights and sounds. Your job is not to tell your readers *about* the things you see and hear but to make it possible for your readers to see and hear these things for themselves.

CHECKPOINT 4

Choose which of the pair in each of the following items would make the more interesting subject for a P.I.A. story:

1. the handsome, agreeable boy who is known and liked by almost everybody for his engaging personality, or the rude loner who spends every spare minute trying to build a motorcycle out of junk scavenged from the dump

2. a bank teller who builds a violin, or a bank president who buys a Rolls Royce

3. the tough old lady who runs the corner newsstand, or the wealthy widow who takes a world cruise

4. the raucous tomboy who pickets the home of the baseball coach because he won't allow girls to play on the team, or the girl with the wealthy parents who spends every winter break in Acapulco

5. a girl who races motorcycles, or a girl who takes flying lessons

6. an agreeable college professor, or a disagreeable politician

7. a boy who drives an expensive foreign car to school, or a boy who works in an auto repair shop

Be prepared to supply good reasons to back up your choice in each case.

The Fine Art of Hanging Around

Regardless of the person you select as the subject for a P.I.A. story, you must make it clear to that person immediately that it will be necessary for you to maintain contact for a considerable period. A genuine P.I.A. story requires more than a cut-and-dried question-and-answer session over doughnuts and coffee. Your goal, remember, is to observe a personality *in action*. That means you've got to be where the action is—and stay there long enough to get a thorough look at it.

As you may have observed in the Bill Murphey P.I.A. story, the kind of information that appears in such a story is impossible to pick up simply by asking questions. This kind of story requires you to hang around as much as possible while your subject is in action—not merely answering questions, but moving around, talking, responding naturally to your questions as they naturally come up. Above all, your subject must be *doing* something that you can observe during the interview.

Obviously, you must ask questions during this observation

105

period, including factual questions: "When did you . . . ? Where did you . . . ?" "What . . . ? Why . . . ? How . . . ?" These questions will cover the facts you need for your story (a good P.I.A. story must always be based solidly on facts). But bear in mind always, when you are interviewing your subject, that you are not there merely to ask questions. You are there as an *observer*. And part of your job is to stay in the background as much as possible, soaking up sounds, colors, movement, gestures, voice tones, and above all, specific details of every kind—everything, in short, that will help your future reader see, hear, and understand the kind of person you are writing about.

It might take several meetings to get a full picture. When your subject is busy doing whatever it is that he or she does, you should be on the scene, watching the action. If your subject is a boy who works on cars, that could mean bending over a balky motor, getting a little grease on your own elbows, fetching tools, listening to what is said (and exactly how it's said), getting the names of things, learning the lingo. If your subject is on the track team, it could mean running a lap or two to get a real sense of what it's like, mingling with the team, listening to track talk, picking up the lingo. If your subject is the female lead in the class play, it could mean watching her rehearse, listening to the backstage chatter, rapping with the stage crew, learning the lingo.

If you choose to write your P.I.A. story about an adult, the game is the same, whether your subject is a laborer, an office worker, an athlete, a politician, or a rod-riding drifter. You visit the excavation site or the office or the dressing room or the campaign headquarters or the railyards, you watch the action, you make note of the colors you see and of specific details that catch your eye, you listen to the sound, and—again—you pick up the lingo.

The things people talk about and the way they talk about them offer insights into their personalities. So do a host of other things: the environment they move around in, the private space they occupy, the things they handle, the clothes they wear, the way they move, the vocabulary they use, their opinions on everything connected with their main interests. As the writer of a P.I.A. story, you are in search of all these things—of everything, in short, that makes your chosen subject visible, audible, active, real.

Reality. That's what you are after in a P.I.A. story. That means hanging around, catching the scene, soaking up impressions and details until you have a full sense of your subject's personality in action.

Most people who are being interviewed enjoy this. They like the fact that you are interested enough to observe and listen. Occasionally you may find somebody who tells you to shove off, but that's extremely rare—and when it happens, it's another key to character, so you have really lost nothing (the refusal to be interviewed might be the source of another story). The one thing you must guard against, constantly, is the temptation to start telling your subject what *you* think, thus turning the occasion into a social chat or an argument rather than an interview.

Stay in the background when you interview your subject. Ask questions, of course, but not pointless questions designed to pass the time or merely to appear friendly. Keep your own personality in check. Don't argue, don't criticize, don't intrude, don't mouth off, don't try to impress anybody, don't call attention to yourself in any way, and don't pass judgment on what you see and hear. You are not there to pass judgment. You are there as an uninvolved observer whose job it is to look, to listen, to collect information, to understand what you see and hear—and to call as little attention to yourself as possible.

Obviously, when you finally start writing your story, your own personality will influence what you have to say and the way you say it, but while you are on the scene, your presence should be as inconspicuous as possible. Remember that the story you will write is about the person you interview, not about you.

It's remarkably easy to forget that. To be on the safe side, remind yourself occasionally that your job is to keep your eyes and ears wide open and your mouth firmly shut except for good reason—meaning a reason directly related to getting information for your story.

CHECKPOINT 5

Suppose you decide to write a P.I.A. story about each of the following:

1. a potential All-American football player
2. a grocer who has been robbed
3. a girl in training for the Olympic gymnastic team
4. an old man or woman who refuses to move out of a house that has been condemned to make room for a freeway exit
5. a scientist doing laboratory research on brain function, using white rats
6. a high school student who leaves home to join a religious cult

In each case, assuming that you could get permission to conduct the necessary interviews and that all could be carried out in your hometown, precisely where would you go, what kind of detail would you expect to look for, and what questions might you ask your subject? Compare and discuss your answers to these questions.

This Note-taking Business

Given the huge range of information you must collect to write a P.I.A. story, it's absurd to assume that you can do the job without taking notes. The question is not whether to take them but what, precisely, should you take note of during your interview. The answer to that is exceedingly simple: Everything.

Everything? Well, almost everything. You need a little practice to get the sense of just how it's done, but once you have tried the P.I.A. method, you will understand its value, for it will almost certainly make an instant change for the better in your writing. Follow all the forthcoming instructions exactly.

Before leaving for your P.I.A. interview (which will of course take place wherever your subject is doing whatever he or she does), arm yourself with plenty of cheap writing paper. An old newspaperman's trick is to fold several sheets of newsprint together, accordion-style, thus creating a long, narrow pad that is easy to hold in the hand and to flip over when a fresh writing space is needed. Arm yourself also with at least two soft-lead pencils or ballpoint pens. Pencils break. Pens go dry. Take no chances.

When you begin the actual interview, make a brief written notation not only of the answers to any questions you ask but of *everything* that attracts your attention even momentarily. Colors. Sounds. Textures. Objects. Facial expressions. Movements. Jot down a word or two about everything you actually notice. You don't need long, laborious notes or complete sentences. You won't have time for them in any case. Nor do you have time, while you are scribbling, to decide just what you will find useful or important when you finally sit down to write your story. You may ultimately throw out a third or more of the notes you gather. But by collecting masses of detail, much more than you can possibly use, you will have a wonderful array of choices available when you start putting your story together.

Do not, however, labor over these notes. Forget about complete sentences. Keep every note brief and write quickly; the more notes you write, the better. Use shortcuts: Try to get every impression down in two or three words. If you see something particularly striking and want to make sure you remember it, use the quickest way possible to make it stand out—exclamation points, maybe, or heavy underlining, or all-capital printing. Is the person you are interviewing a nut on the color green? Write *GREEN!!!* When you see that note later, your memory will pull up enough green items from the scene of the interview to make the notation clear. The same technique will work for just about anything you observe: sounds, shapes, colors, noises, movements, emotions, clothes, ornaments, tools, tones, textures—one or two key words in your notes can bring back a whole vivid complex of remembered things. Your notes will probably make no sense at all to anybody but you. That's fine. They are meant only for you. And they will give you invaluable assistance in the actual business of writing your final paper.

No matter how good your memory is, don't trust it. Take notes. And more notes. Don't worry about whether they are important or not. Just take them.

You can make notes on the casual conversation of your P.I.A. subject in the same way. You need only jot down enough of the actual words spoken to remind you of a complete remark; then you can reconstitute it, using quotation marks, so that it sounds right—that is, like the actual conversation of the person quoted. Note, however, that this method is acceptable only for casual remarks. If the person you are interviewing makes a statement of fact or expresses a strongly held opinion, you must be strictly accurate in your quotation. In addition, you must always double-check with the person you are quoting to make certain that you have not twisted the facts or misrepresented the opinion in any way whatever.

Never, under any circumstances, put words in the mouth of your interviewee unless they were actually spoken. And, of course, as a matter of common sense, don't quote your subject just to be quoting; any comments you use should either supply a reader with some kind of information about your interviewee or reveal some aspect of personality or character.

CHECKPOINT 6

This is a trial run. Its whole point is to give you experience with fast, comprehensive note-taking. You will serve once as the interviewer, once as interviewee.

Draw a classmate's name out of a hat and present yourself as a newspaper or magazine writer who wants an interview. Find out what particular subject or school activity is of the greatest interest to your interviewee, and focus your attention on it: what the interest is, the kind of activity or study it involves, how much time it takes, how it has affected the interviewee's thinking or plans for the future, and so on.

While you are taking notes on this information, make note also of the following:

1. the age, sex, and physical appearance of your subject, including style of dress and characteristics of body movement and speech.

2. several "close-up" details of the place where the interview is held (if it's held in the classroom, fine; your notes should reflect this).

3. at least one direct statement that you could quote in writing.

After you have finished your interview, reverse roles. If you were interviewed the first time around, act this time as interviewer. (It's best to work with a different partner when you switch roles.)

Since the whole point of this interview is to give you practical note-taking experience, it is essential that you take your notes as though you actually intend to write a complete story. You will not be required to do this, but you will need your notes for one further checkpoint, so hang on to them.

Checking Out Your Stash

How to sort out the huge jumble of fragmentary notes jotted down for a P.I.A. story into some kind of comprehensible framework can't be reduced into any standard formula. Only one thing is certain: The bigger your stash of notes, the better. Almost certainly you won't use them all. But that's not the point. The point is that the more you have, the greater the possibility that you will find just what you need to produce a story that is alive and interesting.

You have probably already formed a private first impression of your subject. Nevertheless, read over your notes—*all* of them. First impressions are not always accurate. And no matter how fragmentary your notes are, or how crazily jumbled they look, they will help you "distance" your subject—that is, to look over quietly, without any sense of personal pressure, all the information you have gathered.

Almost invariably this process results in new insights and a strengthened visualization of everything you have observed. Best of all, it tends to start an automatic sorting-out process in your mind: you will begin to see what you can use most effectively, what will "work" in the written story and what won't. Almost everybody has a subconscious sense of story. Give yours a chance to start working for you: Feed it those notes.

CHECKPOINT 7

Study the notes you wrote for your trial-run P.I.A. story until they are completely familiar to you. Pick out at least three notes (more if you like) that contain one or more of the following:

    1. a specific color
    2. a specific texture (silk, wool, wood, steel, leather, cotton, fur, whatever)
    3. a specific sound other than a voice
    4. any small, specific object handled by or worn by the interviewee
    5. specific words actually spoken by the interviewee

Work all these elements into two or three paragraphs of connected narrative. Don't worry about creating a finished product. The point of this exercise is to help you get the feel of converting written notes into connected narrative.

And Now the Real World

It's time now to put the techniques you have studied into action with somebody outside your ordinary school environment. Choose an adult as the subject of a P.I.A. story, and request an interview. Don't be shy about this. Most adults will be delighted to cooperate. Look around your neighborhood or town for any likely subject—grocer, plumber, waitress, news vendor, baker, lumberjack, cook, designer, taxi driver, gardener, construction worker, nurse, telephone operator, garbage collector, mechanic, police officer, dog trainer. Almost anybody will do, provided the person you choose has some kind of job or special activity and is *not* somebody you know well.

It is best not to choose as your subject any person in the white-collar professions. Professional people make poor subjects for two reasons: (1) They are often reluctant to take the necessary time for a full interview, and (2) they are seldom as colorful or as interesting to write about as people who work mainly with their hands. You can carry on an interview with a mechanic or a dog trainer, for example, while the actual work of mechanical repair or dog training is going on, a process that offers you a rich supply of colorful detail to use in your writing. You can't carry on an interview with a lawyer who is trying to write a brief or with a bookkeeper who is working on a ledger. If you can possibly manage it, find yourself an interviewee whose work requires the use of muscle as well as mind.

Once you nail down a prospect for your P.I.A. story, including permission to hang around as an observer long enough to collect all the information you need, set a date with your subject at his or her workplace—whatever that is. Prepare yourself in advance with several questions you want to ask. Other questions will occur to you during your hanging-around period, but you need a few to get started. Show up at the appointed time. And focus all your energies from that time forward on observing, listening, and taking notes on *everything* you see and hear, paying particular attention to tools or equipment of any kind, to unusual sounds, to colors, and to shoptalk. (Refer again to pages 108-110 for note-taking tips.)

You should wind up with a great disorganized jumble of notes that will make very little sense to anybody except yourself. Read over all those notes *immediately*. Don't wait until the next day. (By the next day, you may have forgotten what you meant by that asterisk or huge capital letter or high-speed scrawl that was meant to be a word.) *Read all your scribbled notes immediately,* and type them on clean paper if possible. If that's not possible, at least fill in any blanks in your notes and make all the words legible; only thus can you be sure you will be able to read them the next day. (Don't trust your memory; the road to held-up assignments is paved with beliefs in good memory.)

After you have read over your notes and put them in readable condition, you can lay them aside until the next day. But not before. No matter how tired, bored, sleepy, or exasperated you feel, read over those notes immediately after your interview.

CHECKPOINT 8

You now have in your hands a complete set of notes from your P.I.A. interview. *Study those notes.* Pay particular attention to two things: (1) any conversation you have noted between the person you interviewed and any other person (not yourself), and (2) any action connected with your interviewee's job (a mechanic, for example, might crawl under a car, a grocer might open a crate of bananas). A scrap of real conversation that is related to the interviewee's job, or any real action thus related, can supply you with an introductory scene for your P.I.A. story. What you have is precisely what the opening scene of a drama has: setting, action, dialogue.

Write this scene, not in the form of a drama but simply as a true story of what you saw and heard. Hang on to all your notes. You will need them again.

Staying Out of Sight

By its very nature, a P.I.A. story represents a completely individual point of view. As the writer, you show the reader what *you* see, as *you* see it. Your presence permeates every sentence. It cannot be otherwise; everything you have ob-

114

served is filtered through your senses. At first glance, therefore, it might seem perfectly logical to write your P.I.A. story in first person. But is it? Compare the following examples:

First Person	Third Person
The old man showed me his collection of rocks, which he told me he had been collecting for years.	The old man likes to show visitors his rock collection, a hobby that started forty years ago when he stumbled upon his first agate on a fishing trip with his father.
I asked Johnny whether he had played basketball in grade school, and he told me he got his start in the sixth grade with a team called the Raiders.	Johnny started playing basketball in the sixth grade. "We called ourselves the Raiders," he says. "We were a tough outfit. We played the fifth grade eleven times and won once."

Obviously, all those *I*'s and *me*'s are unnecessary. And if you want to write a successful P.I.A. story, you should start training yourself immediately in the observance of one rule about using the first-person pronoun in such stories.

In a word: *Don't.*

Why not? For some very good reasons, including first and foremost, this one: The story you write is *by* you; it is not *about* you. It is about the person you have chosen as your subject, and if you are to do that person justice, you must give him or her absolute center stage. As soon as you allow yourself to use the first-person pronoun, you run the risk of taking your reader's attention away from your real subject and centering it on yourself. This may do lovely things for your ego, but it will infuriate your readers. After all, they know you're there, behind the written words, and they are perfectly aware that it is your voice they hear coming off the page. And they will listen to you happily so long as you don't keep pushing your *I-me-my-mine* in their faces. As soon as you do that, the party's over. Readers will put you down as a klutz on an ego trip. Not fair, because you didn't mean it that way? Maybe so. That's what happens, nevertheless.

Observe in the following contrasting examples how easily that annoying pronoun sinks out of sight:

> I knew that Kate was a real expert with automobile engines, so I asked her where she had learned her skill. She told me that when she was 12 years old her father had an old truck that was always breaking down, so she would try to fix it. I asked, "Did your father teach you a lot?" She replied that she did this without her father's knowledge. I got the impression that her father was very strict.

> Kate got her start as a mechanic early. "Pop had this old green pickup that broke down about every other day," she said. "A '68 Ford. So I started fooling around with it. Strictly on the Q.T., of course. I was only about 12, and I figured Pop would really burn my behind if he caught me messing around with that truck. He would have, too." She laughed. "I got me a lot of rides out of that old clinker while he thought it was laid up."

By requiring yourself to write entirely in third person, thus vanishing from the scene, you will be able to keep your subject in much better focus. Your whole writing style will therefore almost certainly improve. It will become clearer, sharper, and—oddly enough—more distinctively and pleasingly "you" precisely because you have removed that annoying first-person pronoun.

It is particularly important to remain invisible in a P.I.A. story. As the writer, you are present strictly as an observer, not as a character in the story. If you insist upon injecting yourself into the picture by way of the first-person pronoun, you run the risk of sounding self-important, silly, or both. Bear that in mind whenever the temptation to fall back on those *I-me-mines* becomes overwhelming. Not only do you not need them; you are better off without them.

CHECKPOINT 9

The following example is infested with first-person pronouns. Remove all of them, and rewrite the paragraph in third person, using appropriate dialogue and replacing as many generalities as possible with highly specific detail. Work in at least one color. Add anything you like to make the paragraph more "seeable" and "hearable" for the reader, but don't change the meaning of the paragraph.

> When I interviewed Mr. Dalby, the school custodian, I asked him how long he had worked at Wahtega High. He told me he had been with the school for twenty-seven years, four months, and three days. I asked him if the students seemed any different now. He made it clear that he certainly thought they were different. However, I got this impression more from his manner than his words. At this point he turned his back on me and walked away, and I was unable to get any further statement from him. He acted quite peculiar, in my opinion.

Making Connections

One of the great values of the action scene used as the opening for a P.I.A. story is the perfectly natural way such a scene can move on immediately into the hard information required for the story—facts, figures, background information of every kind. If you recall the sample P.I.A. story on page 94, represented here with the opening scene and its follow-up, you can see how it works.

> "Hey, Murph!" The voice is loud and male, and it's coming from an upstairs room in a posh house in one of the poshest subdivisions in the city. "How about checkin' me out? I'm through up here."
> "Hey, Murph!" Another male voice, this time from the living room. "You wanna look at this stain on the rug? It wasn't here last time."
> "Hey, Murph!" It's the upstairs voice again. "Hold the checkout. I need another ten minutes."
> Murph himself, William B. Murphey, senior at John Nelson High School and current runner-up for the state high school wrestling championship (148-lb. class), is finishing up his work in the kitchen. He is dressed in an ancient pair of jeans, an equally ancient sweatshirt, and a pair of snow-white socks. He has just finished scrub-

117

bing the floor, and he is walking across it now, rubbing it with his feet, stopping to look every few steps at the soles of his socks. They are still clean. He looks pleased.

After the opening paragraphs, the writer begins to present straightforward facts that readers need to know in order to establish more firmly in their minds the identity of the subject. This factual presentation should begin immediately after the opening scene; otherwise, readers will lose interest very rapidly. They will enjoy a brief glimpse of the personality in action, but unless it is backed up very quickly with hard information, they will begin to wonder, irritably, just who it is you are writing about, and why.

Once you have firmly established the identity of your subject with straightforward facts, you can jump back to your opening scene and continue it with other material gathered during your observation period. No rule of thumb can govern the arrangement of your material. Your notes will dictate to a large extent just when and where to use any particular piece of information. You can determine very quickly where that information will make the most sense, be most effective, or simply sound right. Generally speaking, your best guide is a commonsense consideration of what is most likely at any given point to hold the interest of a reader or to meet the reader's need for information.

As you put your story together, ask yourself the same questions a reader (or a listener) would probably be asking. After your opening action scene those questions are likely to be these: "Just exactly who is this person I'm reading about? What's special about him or her? How old is he or she? What's he or she really like?"

If you do a thorough job of note-taking during your hanging-around period, the answers to all such questions are already in your hands. Among those notes you will have not only all sorts of personal impressions, colorful detail, and bits of conversation but a great deal of solid information— plain hard facts, in other words.

Without this tough core of solid information, a P.I.A.

story will be weak and uninteresting, no matter how vivid the writer's personal style. You cannot omit this material, nor can you distort it by dressing it up with fancy or cutesy-pie language in the hope of holding a reader's interest. Factual material must always be completely accurate. It is not necessary, however, to throw such information at your readers in big, indigestible chunks. So how do you handle it?

Answer: Forthrightly. First, evaluate the importance of your facts. If they are necessary to a reader's clear understanding of your story, they must be included. And they will fit smoothly into your narrative if, as you write, you think like a reader, thus anticipating what your reader will want to know and supplying it at the right time.

In large measure, plain common sense will dictate just where and when to include various kinds of straight factual material. Perhaps the best way to get the whole business clear in your mind, however, is to think of your P.I.A. story as a motion-picture documentary. This will enable you to move smoothly and easily from action scenes and pictorial details (all the things that could actually be captured on film) to factual material that would be handled, in a documentary, as voice-over.

Ask yourself these questions as you write your P.I.A. story: "If I were filming this, what exactly would I photograph? Where would I need a voice-over to explain the meaning of any picture or to add facts that can't be filmed [dates, place names, historical references, biographical notes, any kind of necessary explanatory material]?"

Once you begin to think of your work in this way—as a filmed documentary—your P.I.A. story will tend to fall automatically into a pattern that will be simultaneously clear and interesting to a reader.

CHECKPOINT 10

Paste or tape together three sheets of lined notebook paper so that they form one very wide sheet of horizontal lines (what you will have, in effect, is a set of three wide columns lined up together). Write the following headings on the pages:

On page 1: Action Scene
On page 2: Specific Visible Details and Audible Sounds
On page 3: Actual Speech

Then enter appropriate notes from your on-scene collection under each of the headings. The notes must be lined up in the proper relation to each other, so that you can see at a glance what you would photograph or place on a soundtrack at any given time. What you will have, in effect, is a shooting script for a documentary. The only difference is that you will be using words rather than film to show in action the personality you have chosen to write about.

Leave plenty of space between each entry on each of your lists. You will need it for additional notes and assorted reminders when you begin working on the final draft of your story. Don't start working yet on this final version. You need to know something about the final step in the P.I.A. process before you proceed.

The Closing Scene

In effect, you now have in your hands a scenario—everything a film director would need to make a documentary—and therefore everything you will need as a writer to write a full-fledged P.I.A. story, except for one thing. Your story still needs a conclusion, an ending that seems to wrap up the whole story in some way, giving it a satisfying sense of completeness.

The conclusion of a P.I.A. story, like the introduction, often stymies a writer. There you are, with masses of material, all kinds of action, facts, quotations, specific details, color, and sound. Yet you feel helpless in the face of the question, How do I end this thing? How do I leave the reader with a firm sense of mission completed, *finis,* The End?

No one way is always the right way, of course. But the most effective, by far, is a return to the action scene that opens the story. This is not always possible, but very often it is both possible and simple. You need only cut back to that first scene, as though all the written words between have been merely a long interruption, and *show* the person you are writing about one more time, still doing whatever it is that he or she does that you found interesting enough to write about. In other words, close your story with a last glimpse of your subject actually *doing* something clearly connected with that first opening scene.

If, as sometimes happens, you cannot logically return to that opening scene, your next best choice is another action scene of some kind involving your subject. The point, in other words, is to *show* your reader a final picture of the person you have interviewed, either doing something or speaking, or both.

The important thing is to leave your reader, at the end of your story, with a final picture of your subject *in action*. Kate, for example (page 116), might be changing a tire on a 1970 Pontiac, or scrounging the junkyard for usable parts. Or working part-time as a mechanic in an auto repair shop. Or bending over the motor of her Uncle Egbert's ancient Studebaker. What you show her doing in your story depends entirely on Kate herself. *What she does is what you write.* You can't make it up. Your final scene, like all others, must be something you have actually observed.

If for any reason you feel, after writing your conclusion, that it's not quite right, perhaps not "final" enough, another choice is still open: to go again to see the person you interviewed. Whatever this person is doing during your visit, *no matter what it is,* can provide you with a genuinely final scene. Your subject may be as intensely involved as ever in some special project, may have dropped it for some new interest, or may have turned listless and indifferent to any kind of personal goal. All you need to do is *show the reader* what the scene actually is, and you will have your conclusion. The scene *is* the conclusion.

A word of warning: Under no circumstances should you end a P.I.A. story with the kind of formal summary or wrap-up that characterizes a formal essay or with an attempt to point a moral. If any kind of moral lesson is involved in your story, do your readers the courtesy of allowing them to discover it for themselves. To do otherwise is bad taste, bad manners, and bad writing.

Enough said. Now get ready to shoot the works.

CHECKPOINT 11

Using the script you put together for Checkpoint 10 as a guide, write a complete P.I.A. story, ending with a final action scene. Follow your scenario scene by scene, incorporating into each scene all the action, specific visual details (in color) and audible sounds, and actual spoken language that you outlined earlier.

Your goal is to make your story as visible and as audible as it would be in a filmed documentary, without using motion-picture terms or referring in any way to motion-picture techniques. These are your *secret* weapons, designed for one purpose: to make your writing more interesting. Letting your reader in on your secrets of technique would be disastrous. Remember also that you are writing a *connected* narrative, so don't rely on pictures and sounds alone. You must connect all these pictures, sounds, and facts in language that will make perfect sense to a reader.

End your story with either a return to your very first scene for a final picture and/or additional dialogue, or with a different, final action scene. Use whichever seems to work better.

Last, but not least, give your story a title, write it at the top of the first page, and under the title, write your name.

Looks pretty good up there, doesn't it?

Index

123

124

126

127